Losing the Fight
against Crime

Losing the Fight against Crime

RICHARD KINSEY

JOHN LEA

JOCK YOUNG

Basil Blackwell

© Richard Kinsey, John Lea and Jock Young 1986
First published 1986

Basil Blackwell Ltd
108 Cowley Road, Oxford OX4 1JF, UK

Basil Blackwell Inc.
432 Park Avenue South, Suite 1503,
New York, NY 10016, USA

British Library Cataloguing in Publication Data

Kinsey, Richard
    Losing the fight against crime.
    1. Crime prevention——Great Britain
    I. Title   II. Lea, John   III. Young, Jock
    364.4'0941   HV7431

    ISBN 0-631-13719-X
    ISBN 0-631-13721-1 Pbk

Library of Congress Cataloging in Publication Data

Kinsey, Richard.
    Losing the fight against crime.
    Bibliography: p.
    Includes index.
    1. Police——Great Britain.   2. Police administration——
Great Britain.   3. Crime and criminals——Great Britain.
I. Lea, John.   II. Young, Jock.   III. Title.
HV8195.A3K56   1986   363.2'0941   85-30790

    ISBN 0-631-13719-X
    ISBN 0-631-13721-1 (pbk.)

Typeset by Freeman Graphic, Tonbridge, Kent
Printed in Great Britain by The Bath Press Ltd, Avon

Contents

Acknowledgements

When we first sat down to write this book we thought it should be fairly straightforward. As it turned out it was not. Very suddenly, both in public and in private, we found ourselves drawn into what, for us at least, were new problems and arguments. We found ourselves talking as academic criminologists with council tenants and community groups, with local labour parties and trades unions – especially the miners – and with a whole spectrum of organizations and individuals outside establishment academic audiences. How do we thank them all?

It is easier to thank our friends and colleagues at the Centres for Criminology at Edinburgh and Middlesex. Beverley Brown, David Garland, Peter Young and Roger Mathews took time to read and talk through the manuscript at different stages. In particular, Derek McClintock will recognize some of our arguments for his own.

Much of the empirical work discussed in the book was financed by the Merseyside Metropolitan Council, which, by the time this book is published, will have ceased to exist. Thankfully Mrs Thatcher will find it impossible to abolish Margaret Simey and John George as she did the Police Committee, on which they played such an important role; nor can she take away the immense help and support given by Peter Gill, Jeff Willis and Peter Turner during our work on the Merseyside Crime Survey. To them and others in Merseyside

– especially Les Moran, Mike Brogden, Peter Goodrich and the Phil – our thanks and best wishes. Special thanks for his unstinting work and advice on the Merseyside Crime Survey must go to Douglas Wood of Social and Community Planning Research. So many people gave freely of their time and help in different ways. Sarah Benton of the *New Statesman*, Mike Davis of the *Chartist*, James Freeman at the *Glasgow Herald* and Jim Seaton at the *Scotsman* commented on ideas which, along the way, appeared first in their papers. Discussions with Martin Kettle at the *Guardian* and Robbie Dinwoodie at the *Scotsman* have been invaluable to us. We owe much to Kate Painter for discussing with us her present research on burglary, to discussions with Alan Phipps on victim surveys, to Jerry Chambers and Sue Miller for their work on sexual assaults and to Duncan Campbell for answering so many of our questions when others with an interest in policing were giving him a very hard time indeed.

Trevor Jones and Walter Easey at the police committee support units at Islington and Camden Councils and our colleagues in the Scottish Council for Civil Liberties gave political and moral support. Rob Baldwin, Steve Box, Dave Cowell, Paddy Hillyard, Neil MacCormick, John Pitts and Jackie Tombs helped more than we had a right to expect.

Introduction

The failure of Mrs Thatcher's law and order programme is plainly visible. The Conservatives claim to be the natural party of law and order, yet since they returned to power in 1979 reported crime has gone up by almost 40 per cent. The rise in crime is only matched by the rising cost of policing Britain. We have a police force that costs every man, woman and child in this country £58 a year. In inner-city areas like Merseyside this rises to £71, and in London it is a staggering £117 per person per year.

Certainly we now have better paid, better qualified, more heavily equipped and greater numbers of police officers than at any time in British history. There are almost twice as many police officers as there were in 1939, and the estimated annual budget for policing England and Wales in 1984–5 was almost £3,000 million. Yet despite this enormous expenditure, the police are more inefficient than they were immediately after the last war. Conservative government policies have not even scratched the surface of the gross ineffectiveness and inefficiency of the police. Each year the proportion of offences cleared up declines inexorably – 41 per cent in 1979, 37 per cent in 1983 and 35 per cent in 1984. And this, of course, includes many offences comparatively simple to detect. For those crimes which involve investigative skills the outlook is even more bleak. In 1951 the official clear-up rate for burglary in England and Wales was 40 per cent by 1984 it had fallen to

28 per cent. In 1984 in London the clear-up rate for burglary was a mere 10 per cent. Perhaps there is no figure which sums up the failure of crime control better than the number of crimes known to the police but not cleared up: the crimes that were successful. For every 100 unsolved crimes in 1979, there were, by 1984, 186. The rate of crime has shot up, but the rate of increase in unsolved crimes has been even more dramatic.

To attempt to shore up an ineffective police force the Conservative government has poured money into an equally ineffective prison service. We have the highest prison population in our history – 47,000 – and the distinction of having more people in prison than any other European country. A monument to the present government is the largest prison-building programme undertaken this century, aiming to provide 16 new gaols and 7,700 new places by the 1990s. The intention was to cope with a predicted 48,500 inmates by 1993, but this figure has almost been reached already. A total of £350 million is to be spent. Yet every realistic analysis of imprisonment has shown that incarceration rates tend to grow to fill the prison accommodation available. It is interesting that in Australia and the Netherlands – and indeed in Britain between 1908 and 1938 – rising crime was accompanied by *decreasing* prison populations.

The problem is not just one of value for money and of statistics. Britain in the 1980s faces a crime problem and a crisis in policing that are unique in the history of the country. For much of the nineteenth century crime was unregulated and the country barely policed. Today Britain is heavily policed and yet still crime is barely controlled. Politicians of all shades periodically acknowledge that there is a problem, but their responses range from the tried, tested and failed formulas of the right – more police with wider powers and tougher prison sentences – to an ageing millenarianism on the left which discounts the present and dreams of a future where the law, the state, capitalism and crime magically wither away. In short, there is a dearth of ideas and an isolation from the harsh realities of crime and policing.

Mrs Thatcher tells us that crime is unrelated to unemployment and poverty. She shuts her eyes to the economic apartheid which now divides the north from the Home Counties and the outer council estates from affluent Finchley. The insurance companies know better. In inner-city Liverpool in 1986 one home in four will be broken into, and one in ten people will have their homes or persons searched by the police. So the building societies will not lend on their houses, the insurance companies double their premiums, and on top of that local government spending is strangled by Westminster.

But has the Labour Party fared any better? There is still a strong belief within all sections of the party that the problem of crime is much exaggerated and that it is rather the fear of crime – generated by the media and the police – that is the real problem. This is an attitude now shared and encouraged by the Home Office. Thus *The British Crime Survey* (Hough and Mayhew 1983) pointed out that the 'statistically average person' is likely to be mugged only 'once every five centuries', burgled 'once in forty years' and assaulted and 'injured however slightly, once every hundred years'. We are told that the risks 'of these fairly serious crimes are small ones'.

As became clear in the wake of the miners' strike of 1984–5, this attitude is readily translated by sections of the Labour left into demands for protection from the police, while the equal need for effective protection from crime is ignored. Such a view sits very easily alongside the unfounded but common belief, especially within the Parliamentary Labour Party, that questions of law and order are dangerously divisive as far as the working class is concerned. Such fears among many Labour MPs reflect tacit and contradictory stereotypes of their constituents as either aggressively anti-police or unfortunately reactionary and in favour of capital punishment.

In some parts of the country, however, Labour-controlled police authorities have taken a more positive stance. in February 1984 we were commissioned by Merseyside Metropolitan Council to conduct a survey of crime and policing within the county. Costing £94,000, it was the first major local survey of its kind in this country. Over 3,500 people were interviewed out of the total population of 1.5 million. The object was to find out what people want from the police and what type of service they are getting. The results present a particularly bleak picture of the problem of crime for working-class people, and point to significant weaknesses and omissions in Labour Party policy.

On an issue bedevilled with assumptions and assertions and precious few facts, the Merseyside survey asked who suffers most from different household and personal crimes, who are the most worried about such offences, who are the most vulnerable, and what they want from the police. Across Merseyside – and, we can safely assume, in other areas of the country – crime is seen to be the third biggest social problem; only unemployment and the lack of facilities for children and young people are more pressing. Thus 35 per cent of people see crime as a 'big problem' in their area – ahead of housing (17 per cent), schools (4 per cent), and race relations (1 per cent). In inner-city areas in Liverpool and Birkenhead crime moves into second place, outranked only by unemployment.

It is too easy to attribute such anxieties to media-generated moral panics set in train by the over-reaction of the propertied middle-classes. Far from it: the more likely you are to be a victim of crime in Merseyside, the more worried you will be about it. And the more worried, the poorer and more vulnerable you actually are. In the outlying wealthy suburbs, such as Ainsdale and Birkdale, only 13 per cent see crime as a major problem, by comparison with 66 per cent in parts of inner-city Liverpool. Crime is far from being a rare event here. A full 44 per cent of people interviewed in Merseyside had been victims of crime in the 12 months before our interview, and a quarter had been victims on two or more occasions. Further, the incidence of crime varied with wealth – for example, multiple victimization (that is, having been a victim more than once in the previous year) is twice as high in the inner-city as in the affluent suburbs. The poor not only suffer crime more often, but the impact on them is much more severe. One third of those living in the poorest council estates described the impact of crimes they had suffered as 'very big', as compared to only one in ten of the residents interviewed in the affluent areas.

It needs emphasizing that crime and the fear of crime hit working-class women more than any other major section of society. It is sometimes suggested that such fears are irrational, as women run less risk of victimization than men. In terms of the Merseyside results, this is not so. First, the actual chances of being a victim of crime are almost the same for men and for women – men under 30 being the exception, largely because of the high rate of interpersonal violence among young males. This general similarity of victimization rates for men and for women is despite the fact that women take much more elaborate precautions against crime than men do. Secondly, women suffer sexual and general harassment on the streets to a far greater extent than men. In some parts of the inner-city, for example, half of all women under 50 interviewed said that they had been 'upset' by such incidents during the last year. To these findings of the Merseyside survey we should add that, as *The British Crime Survey* (Hough and Mayhew 1983) showed, women are particularly vulnerable to certain types of crime, such as bag-snatching. Also, rates of domestic violence and serious sexual assault are considerably greater than most survey techniques can pick up, because of the embarrassment and, in some instances, the fear occasioned by the interview.

If we look at the impact of crime on people's lives, the survey reveals extraordinary effects on the daily lives of the most vulnerable groups. One in five of all respondents said that they *always* avoided going out after dark for fear of crime. In the poorer council estates this rises to one quarter. It reaches a peak in areas of the inner-city, where one person in three said that they 'always' and a further 15 per cent that they 'often' did not go out at night, while 38 per cent reported that they felt unsafe in their own homes. Such is the reality of crime and the depth of its effects. In many inner-city areas and on the outer council estates substantial sections of the population

– women especially – are living under a virtual curfew. That this should be largely ignored by the left is a disgrace forged of dogma and short-sightedness: dogma, because of an aversion to what has come to be seen as a 'Tory issue', and short-sightedness because the majority of those who write, work and make decisions in this area are, like us, white, middle-class and male – largely untouched by crime.

It should not come as a surprise to learn that a vast majority in the Merseyside survey were strongly in favour of greater provision for policing. As many as 90 per cent in some inner-city areas wanted to see more police officers on foot patrol. However, respondents were also very clear about what they wanted the police to be doing. There were three outstanding priorities: the provision of an immediate response to emergencies (90 per cent of respondents cited this), crime investigation (80 per cent) and the maintenance of a deterrent by the presence of officers on the street (74 per cent). But are the police meeting these priorities? Are they giving value for money? We now know, for example, that the massive expenditure on computer technology and intelligence systems has not resulted in better clear-up rates for crime. In London in 1983 – the Metropolitan Police Commissioner Sir Kenneth Newman's 'year of achievement' – the number of crimes cleared up per police officer fell to four per year, at the staggering cost of £5,578 per crime cleared up. What are the police doing with their time and our money? Are separate Criminal Investigation Departments, traffic divisions, Special Patrol Groups and so on, cost-effective? Might we not consider their abolition, thereby releasing officers for uniform patrol work and the investigation of specific offences such as burglary, which at the moment are frequently written off as soon as they are reported?

At present such suggestions are readily dismissed. The police insist on an exclusive right to set the agenda in discussions on police effectiveness. The lack of accountability of police to the public has combined with the failure of the Labour Party to take crime and policing seriously, resulting in the shameful underestimation of the extent of crime as a social problem, especially among those social groups – women, the poor, the unemployed, ethnic minorities – which, above all, Labour must look to and fight for.

In addition, the nature of crime and the impact of victimization are consistently misrepresented in the media. On an average night there are five hours of peak television time given over to crime and police dramas (excluding police and crime-related items on news programmes). Crime headlines are the staple diet of the popular Press and recurrent themes on the radio. From such media coverage one gains the distorted impression that the typical criminal is the ruthless bank-robber and the typical crime the violent theft of a considerable amount of money. If anything, the opposite is true. Most crimes are committed against the working-class poor, and the amounts of money are small: two thirds of burglaries involve losses of under £100. They are committed very often by adolescents who are in no sense devoted to a criminal career; they are amateurish burglaries which occur often on impulse with little planning or forethought. Today's offender will be law-abiding tomorrow, and a victim the day after. The lesson to be learned here is that it is not the individual offence – which is often insignificant by comparison with its dramatized portrayal on the television – but its cumulative effect on the lives of people already harassed and demoralized by all the other familiar problems of the inner-city today. A thousand pin pricks add up to a major laceration. On the other hand there are crimes, notably those committed by men against women, for which the effect of the media is both to distort and to seriously underestimate the impact. Rape is the obvious example in which the consistent tenor of the media is to blame the victim – women are seen as in reality inviting the offence – or to laugh off its impact on an individual's life, as is so often the case with sexual harassment of all kinds.

The image of the police is likewise distorted by the media. The counterpart of the ruthless bank-robber is the cynical yet dedicated and successful detective. The police are frequently portrayed as the 'thin blue line', our last resort against the rising tide of lawlessness – and against whom criticism amounts to treachery. There is of course an element of truth somewhere behind this rhetoric. Between 1971 and 1981 the number of police officers rose by 23 per cent, whereas the number of offences reported to the police rose by 78 per cent. This in part explains the decline in the clear-up rate: police officers simply have a much bigger workload. But what it does not explain is why the absolute number of crimes cleared up per police officer is so low in the first place (9.5 per annum), nor the staggering cost of the exercise. Any private enterprise with such disastrously low productivity would have gone to the wall long ago; it certainly would not have received regular subsidies and support from a Conservative government.

In part the crisis in policing is a crisis in management. There surely has to be something amiss when a police constable spends more time in the police canteen each day than in interviewing witnesses, suspects and informants. Yet this was the finding of both the Policy Studies Institute study of the London Metropolitan Police and our own survey of the Merseyside police. As the Policy Studies Institute report put it, 'it seems extraordinary that only 2 per cent of police time is spent on interviewing suspects and witnesses, bearing in mind that this is the most important source of information leading to the apprehension of offenders' (PSI 1983, vol. 3, p. 40).

But the crisis in policing is also rooted in the alienation of the police from those very sections of the community upon which they most depend. Contrary to popular belief, the police only very rarely detect crime or catch criminals by themselves. In order to clear up crime they rely on the public at virtually every stage, from first reporting the offence to standing in court to give evidence. Of course, surveys regularly show that the vast majority of people support the police. The trouble is that these are the people who have least contact with the police, least contact with crime, and therefore least information to give to the police. In inner-city areas where crime is most prevalent and knowledge of crime is at its most extensive, relations between police and public are at their lowest ebb. Indeed, statistically the strongest indicator of whether or not you will be stopped and searched by the police is whether in fact you have been a *victim* of crime.

Of such facts are Mrs Thatcher's two nations composed: the poor, decaying areas where crime is highest and policing is most ineffective albeit intrusive, and the wealthy suburbs with low crime rates and low-profile policing. A disturbing trend is apparent – noted by recent Home Office reports, some chief constables and some sections of the Labour Party. Crime, it is said, is a product of fundamental social and economic problems, of which there are certainly plenty; thus 'any type of policing', as a *Guardian* editorial (25 August 1984) put it, 'can only make a limited impact upon crime'. The Thatcher government is quite capable of using such words of wisdom as a reason for leaving the inner cities to rot – they'll never vote Conservative in any case. Meanwhile, many in the Labour opposition still believe that little can be done until the social and economic conditions which cause crime are eliminated. Both, we hope to show in this book, are wrong.

1

The Crisis in Policing

Crime is increasing. One glance at the almost exponential graph for the growth in crime known to the police in England and Wales alerts us to the gravity of the situation (see Figure 1). The number of crimes known to the police multiplied by over 30 since 1901, by 15 since the 1930s and by six since the last war. Recently the crime rate has grown very rapidly indeed: a 68 per cent increase over the last ten years in England and Wales, a doubling of crimes known to the police in Scotland, and an 80 per cent rise in the London Metropolitan Police area. Of course, we stress that this refers to crime known to the police – the real crime rate, which includes the dark figure of unreported crimes, may have risen less rapidly. *The British Crime Survey*, which directly asked the public the number of crimes committed against them estimated a real rise in burglary of 20 per cent over the period 1972 to 1983, compared to the 100 per cent rise given by the police figures. This discrepancy probably reflects an increase in reporting of crimes because of the growth of insurance; people who have been burgled are now more likely to report theft, whatever they think of the crime being solved. Burglary is obviously particularly likely to be affected in this way.

If we take a wider sample of crimes we find less discrepancy between the police and *Crime Survey* figures. *The British Crime Surveys* of 1981 and 1983 found a 10 per cent increase in crime; a 12 per cent rise is given in police figures (see Hough and

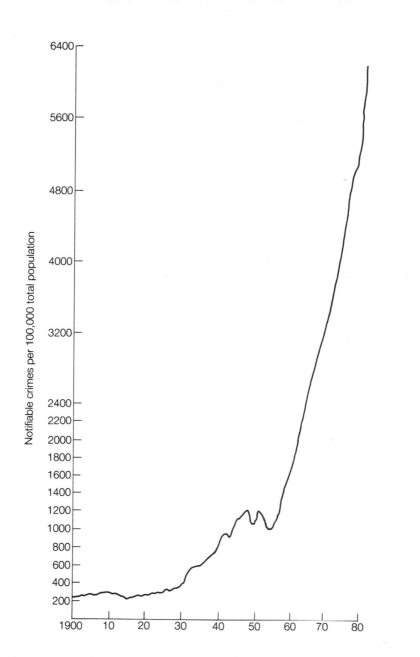

Figure 1   Numbers of notifiable crimes known to the police per 100,000 of the population, England and Wales, 1900–82.

Source: Updated from McClintock and Avison 1968

Mayhew 1985). Moreover, as the majority of crimes known to the police are reported to them by the public, the huge increases in the number of reported crimes indicates a public demand upon the services of the police. The rising rate of crime, together with a steeper rise in demand for police action constitute the core of the problem.

The British police forces face a crisis of considerable proportions – and it is crime which is the motor of this crisis. The problem is magnified in the inner cities, particularly in the metropolitan area of London. It can be seen as having two stages. The first, in the period from 1955 to 1975, was a crisis of effectiveness: an inability ever to catch up with the rising crime rate. The second – what we might term the 'hyper-crisis' – extended from 1975 onwards, when police effectiveness, again particularly in the inner-city areas and with regard to a series of serious crimes, passed below the level at which the police could reasonably be said to be capable of tackling the problem at all.

This stage of the crisis was, ironically, exacerbated by police attempts to overcome the first stage. The introduction of 'unit beat policing' in the 1960s, and the amalgamations and consequent reduction in the number of police forces, coupled with the 'technological revolution' of the 1970s, led only to a heavy reliance upon specialist squads, on the tactics of 'stop and search' and on the 'fire brigade' policing of the 1980s, which saw the speed of response to incidents and 'triple nine' calls as the main index of police efficiency. These changes did not solve the problem of crime control – they only made it worse by weakening the contact between police and community. Further, the crisis has spread out into new areas.

Firstly, there is an increasingly evident crisis in public support for the police. The Policy Studies Institute (PSI 1983) report in London showed that in the areas where policing was already facing problems – in the inner cities – the level of public dissatisfaction was phenomenally high, and reached its greatest among ethnic minorities. Those sections of the population most in need of police protection, and often having most information about crime, were at the same time the most alienated from the police. Furthermore, the same PSI report indicated that large sections of the population believed that there was widespread corruption in the force – a belief fleetingly substantiated by the Operation Countryman investigation into corruption in the Metropolitan Police.

Second, there is the growing crisis in police accountability. In the wake of the inner-city riots of 1981, many commentators including ourselves pointed to the absence of any element of accountability to local government in police policy-making in London. Then, with the miners' strike of 1984–5, the debate on accountability shifted outside London to the provincial forces where, under the 1964 Police Act, county councils and metropolitan counties do have some concern with the administration of policing. The 'tripartite arrangement', whereby the county council is charged with 'maintaining an efficient force' but the chief constable retains all responsibility for 'operational matters', with the Home Secretary functioning as a court of appeal, all but cracked under the strain. Quite apart from the political issues arising from the strike – for example, in relation to the behaviour of some police on the picket lines, and to the emergence of a *de facto* national police force – the distinction between operational matters and maintaining an efficient force disappeared, if indeed it ever existed. The local police authorities, confronted with a rising crime rate and the outbreak of new forms of crime to do with heroin addiction, stood by powerless as large numbers of police officers were shunted off in convoys to the coalfields. The first crisis alone would have necessitated a profound restructuring of the police force. The second, in part brought about, as we have said, by the police attempts to solve the first crisis, cries out for a radical reformulation of the structure and methods of policing.

Despite periodic mobilizations such as that which occurred during the miners' strike, crime control is the central, day-to-day problem that the police have to face, and the preferred activity of the majority of police officers. It is also the central focus of public demand upon the police, the major concern of police 'occupational culture' – the set of beliefs and assumptions in terms of which police officers make sense of their work – and the area where the greatest continuous and cumulative strain on policing has occurred.

Crime control, and the crisis it now faces, offer the key to understanding the vast number and variety of police institutions and practices which have been set up in recent years: Neighbourhood Watch, multi-agency cooperation, large-scale stop and search operations like the 'Swamp 81' excercise which preceded the Brixton riots of that year, community policing, fire brigade policing. Add to these the use made by the police of Home Office research and *The British Crime Survey*, as well as changes in the law such as the recent Police and Criminal Evidence Act. If we are to understand all these initiatives it is vital to look at them in the context of the increasing problems of crime control. Even the innovations in the use of criminal intelligence computer storage and retrieval, which were developed in Northern Ireland in anti-terrorist roles, are redefined in relation largely to crime control when transplanted to mainland Britain.

Let us look at the extent of the problem and the strength of our contention that there is a crisis in crime control.

The Rising Crime Rate

For every 100 crimes known to the police at the outbreak of the Second World War there were 163 in 1950, 263 in 1960, 550 in 1970 and 891 in 1980. This rise is seemingly inexorable, for it has continued both through affluence and through recession. And these numbers have risen much faster than police numbers have. The figures are an index of the demands made on the police by the public with regard to crime. Other demands are, of course, also made, such as those to do with traffic control and accident supervision, and these also will have increased considerably.

Some idea of the increase in pressure on policing can be

gauged by comparing the number of crimes notified to the public with the numbers of police officers. For although the numbers of police have increased steadily over the years, and there was a 23 per cent increase in England and Wales between 1971 and 1981, there has been a much greater rise in crimes known to the police. Perhaps a clearer way of seeing this rise in workload is to consider the number of crimes reported to the police per police officer. In 1961 it was 11, in 1971 17 and by 1981 23 (see Table 1).

Table 1   Number of crimes reported to the police per police officer, England and Wales, 1961–81

	1961	1966	1971	1973	1976	1979	1980	1981
Police (1000s)	75.8	86.9	97.3	99.2	109.5	113.3	117.3	119.5
Crimes (1000s)	871	1316	1666	1657	2136	2377	2521	3988
Crimes per police officer	11	15	17	17	19	21	22	28

Such an increase occurs virtually every year; there is almost an inevitability about it and it represents in London, for instance, an average 29,000 extra cases on the workload every year. It is sometimes suggested that this increase in crime is largely a function of the police having ever-increasing resources and, therefore, registering more crimes. Against this it should be noted that over 90 per cent of serious crimes known to the police are reported to them by the public. Less than 10 per cent are detected by the police themselves (Hough and Mayhew 1984; Mawby 1979; Bottomley and Coleman 1981), and this falls to 5 per cent in the inner cities. The influence of police resources and activity compared with the public reporting of offences on the overall crime statistics over long periods is therefore very limited, despite the police's manifest ability to manipulate the crime rate for specific crimes over short periods.

Thus, what this tremendous growth in crimes known to the police represents is a steady increase in demands from the public. Whether this is because of the public's increased senstitivity to crime so that they now report crimes which they would not have reported previously, or whether it signals a 'real' increase in crime, is neither here nor there. Whatever the explanation – and, as we shall see, both tendencies are undoubtedly at play – the police workload has increased enormously, and the cause lies predominantly with the public and its experience of crime rather than with any desire on the part of the police to expand their own figures. Furthermore, it is important to note that in situations of great public demand there is an increasing tendency on the part of the police to under-register the amount of crime reported. This tendency is not, we shall argue, evenly distributed: it occurs to a greater extent with certain types of crime rather than others, and when certain sorts of people report crimes to the police.

The Clear-Up Rate as an Index of Efficiency

To the layperson the clear-up rate would seem to be an excellent measure of police efficiency. On the face of it, it would seem to measure the proportion of crimes detected by the police and thereby provide an index of the chances of an offender being apprehended. In fact, it is an extremely inefficient yardstick and one which tends to present an over-optimistic estimate of police performance.

One of the most obvious faults in the notion of clear-up rate is that not all crimes are known to the police. For example, *The British Crime Survey* (Hough and Mayhew 1983) has shown that, at most, only one half of burglaries, a quarter of sexual offences and a very small proportion of vandalism are reported to the police. In London only a half of victim incidents investigated by the Policy Studies Institute (PSI) were reported (PSI 1983, vol. 1, p. 76). Thus the amount of unreported crime is sizeable, and so the clear-up rate does not measure the chances of getting away with a crime or, for that matter, police efficiency. The real clear-up rate is considerably lower than the official figure: indeed, a rough estimate would be achieved by halving it. And the greater the size of the dark figure, the more optimistic the official clear-up rate becomes. In reality, a large figure is often, in part, a reflection of the public's lack of confidence in police ability to deal with crime. Thus *The British Crime Survey* found that in over a third of personal offences and a half of household offences, the public did not report them because of their doubts as to the ability or appropriateness of the police to deal with the matter (Hough and Mayhew 1983). In other words, it is *in part* the public's knowledge of police ineffectiveness that artificially boosts clear-up rates.

Nonetheless, the public do report a large number of crimes to the police, as we have seen, and the numbers rise every year. So, allowing for this, are not clear-up rates useful indicators of the efficiency of the police in solving those crimes known to them, that is, indicators of their ability to cope with public demand? But it is not as simple as this. A whole series of police processes and decisions have to be made before the final clear-up rate is reached. These are summarized in Figure 2, which pinpoints the considerable control that the police have over the figures which make up both the numerator and the denominator of the clear-up rate.

In both the 90 per cent of instances where the public make known a crime to the police and the 10 per cent where the police directly witness an offence, the police have to decide whether to register the incident as a possible crime in the form of a 'crime report'. This involves an act of discretion that is sometimes eminently justifiable, and sometimes not. A man may phone the police complaining that a local building firm insists on parking its van outside his house so that he can't

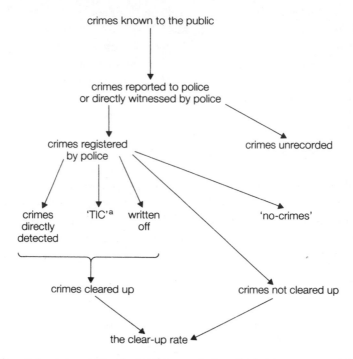

crimes known to the public

crimes reported to police
or directly witnessed by police

crimes registered
by police

crimes unrecorded

crimes
directly
detected

'TIC'ᵃ   written
            off

'no-crimes'

crimes cleared up

crimes not cleared up

the clear-up rate

ᵃ Crimes 'taken into consideration' at the request of an offender.

Figure 2   The construction of the clear-up rate and crimes 'taken into consideration' at the request of an offender.

park his own car there. He thinks it is illegal but, in fact, there is no crime and so no need to register the complaint. Or a fracas occurs outside a public house at closing time and the police are called, but no one is badly hurt. No crime is registered, although one has occurred but is considered too trivial to bother about. Or again, a woman comes into the police station and complains of being assaulted by her husband. The station officer tells her to go away and take a civil action if necessary, but as she has suffered little 'actual bodily harm' there is nothing the police themselves can do. In fact, there is, under Section 47 of the Offences Against the Person Act, even if there has been no bodily harm whatsoever (see Walker

1971, p. 17). The officer does nothing because he fears she will later withdraw the charge, because he thinks the offence is too trivial to bother with and, perhaps, because he doesn't think that police should intervene in domestic disputes. Here, we have started down the road where discretion becomes controversial.

How large is this area of discretion? McCabe and Sutcliffe (1978), in their study of police response to both personal and telephone complaints received at stations in Oxford and Salford, found that in less than half the instances was a crime report actually written. This varied from one in ten of domestic complaints to three quarters of burglaries. And such findings replicate a series of American studies (see summary in Bottomley and Coleman 1981, pp. 64–8). So the discretion level is considerable, both quantitatively and qualitatively. Certain types of crimes committed against certain sorts of people rather than others are less likely to be registered. And even when the offence has been registered in the form of a crime report, a further crucial act of discretion occurs: namely, whether to categorize the incident as a 'crime' or a 'no-crime'. That is, a decision has to be made on whether the incident merits official designation.

The number of no-crimes varies enormously from one police district to another and with the type of offence concerned. For example, Bottomley and Coleman's (1981) sample in a northern industrial city produced an overall 11 per cent of crimes written off as no-crimes, and a variation within offences from 30 per cent of bicycle thefts, to 17 per cent of personal violence, right down to 6 per cent of burglaries. These are considerable figures, occurring as they do after a crime report has already been filled in; however, the scope for discretion here is not as high as with the initial decision of whether to register the offence or to ignore it.

The reasons for the writing-off of public complaints, whether at the initial stage or after a crime report has been filled out, range from the technically obvious and unobjectionable to the discretionary and the controversial. Thus, some incidents will not be crimes at all, and some may be resolved merely by a police officer's presence or by the victim dropping the charge – and here the correct exercise of professional discretion is only to be welcomed. What is worrying, however, are those offences which are dropped because they are technically too difficult (for example, there appears to be insufficient evidence), and those that are a product of an officer's stereotype of 'real crime' or of the level of policing necessary in a certain area. The excuse of technical difficulty, unless carefully checked, may facilitate the tendency to focus on the more easily solvable crimes – which we shall see later is part of police practice and of current thinking. The notion of a 'real crime' may exclude much domestic violence, certain cases of rape or of assault between members of minority groups, or racist assaults upon black people, which the police may ignore.

It is well accepted that the demands on the police of certain sections of the community are taken more seriously than others. Thus R. Sparks et al., when discussing research showing that as many as 28 per cent of cases in Brixton and Hackney were 'no-crimed', while the figure was 18 per cent in Kensington, note that –

almost certainly [the police] handling of reported incidents will vary, according to cultural differences in the community. The treatment of reported incidents in the largely middle-class area like Kensington may well differ for this reason from the treatment of comparable incidents in a mainly lower-class area like Hackney, or in certain parts of Brixton: the 'no-crime' percentages . . . certainly suggest that this is so. (1977, pp. 159–60)

There is little doubt, then, that discrimination occurs in the degree of seriousness attributed particularly to complaints from working class communities and in domestic situations – which to all practical purposes means women – and that this discrimination occurs both before and after the crime report stage. It might be thought that, however wide the police officer's discretion before the point at which investigation proceeds on the basis of the crime report, the reckoning of the clear-up rate after this point must be simple. Isn't the ratio of crimes detected over crimes known? The problem is that clear-up rate is not equivalent to detection rate. An offence 'cleared up' is not necessarily one in which the police have traced a subject who is subsequently prosecuted and convicted. Frequently crimes are 'indirectly' cleared up, that is, the offender asks for other offences to be 'taken into consideration' (TIC). He or she may be presented with a list of offences and asked to admit to them, often in return for more favourable treatment. Even more controversially, if he or she is subsequently acquitted or the prosecution is dropped, the offence may still be regarded as cleared up. Thus we have traced a considerable distance between the notion of clear-up rate and detection rate. All that one can say for sure is that clear-up rates are considerably higher than detection rates. But then this gives us all the more reason to be alarmed at the general decline in the clear-up rates across the country.

The Decline in the Percentage of Crimes Cleared Up

Between 1973 and 1983 the percentage of crimes cleared up by police in England and Wales fell by 10 per cent. In the London Metropolitan Police District the fall was 13 per cent. In Scotland between 1972 and 1982 the clear-up rate fell by 8 per cent. Furthermore, the actual level of clear-ups was already low. In 1983 it stood at 37 per cent for England and Wales and 17 per cent in London. In Scotland in 1983 it was at 31 per cent. Table 2 shows the percentage changes over the period 1973–83 in crimes known to the police, in police manpower and in the clear-up rate. These overall figures of course conceal tremendous differences between the clear-up rates for different types of offence. Crimes which are a product largely of police reaction rather than of public reporting have extremely high clear-up rates: for example, being equipped to steal, or in possession of stolen goods, have clear-up rates of 99 per cent. These are crimes which only become known to the police when the police discover them. Likewise murder, which

Table 2   Changes in rates of crime and police effectiveness,
England and Wales, 1973–83

	% change in the Metropolitan Police	% change in the rest of England and Wales
Crimes known to the police	+86	+85
Police manpower	+28	+22
Clear-up rate	−13	−10
Number of crimes cleared up	+7	+48
Number of crimes not cleared up	+119	+117
Crimes cleared up per police officer	−18	+18

in this country is largely committed by relatives of the victim, and hence the offender is often obvious, has a 97 per cent clear-up rate.

It is crimes which involve the need for extensive detection work which have low clear-up rates. For example, the clear-up rate for burglary in England and Wales in 1983 was 27 per cent, though in the Metropolitan Police District it was a staggering 9 per cent. The Metropolitan Police are exceptionally prone to low and declining clear-up rates. They have the lowest overall clear-up rate of any police force in Britain, and the greatest decline in effectiveness. The contrast here is between national figures which include rural areas with high clear-up rates, and a wholly urban police force. Consider the low standing of the Met in the clear-up league (information from a paliamentary question, Hansard 8 April 1982):

	%
Northumbria	50
South Yorkshire	50
Greater Manchester	41
West Yorkshire	41
Merseyside	34
West Midlands	32
Metropolitan Police District	17

Even if, at the most optimistic assessment, clear-up rates were equivalent to real detection rates, the chances of getting away with crime have never been greater. If we take burglary, for example, and allow for the fact that only a half of offences in many inner-city areas are reported to the police, then the actual clear-up rate is something in the region of 14 per cent. On this reckoning the potential offender would have a 50 per cent higher chance of getting away with burglary than in the 1950s. And one suspects that, as far as the public is concerned, the reporting of the offence to the police owes more to the requirements of insurance claims than to any faith in police detection. The official burglary clear-up rate (for the Metropolitan Police) of 9 per cent is a figure of such low odds that it would scarcely deter the typical opportunist adolescent burglar. If to this we add considerations of social class and area – in inner-city council estates undoubtedly fewer people report burglary to the police – then the detection rate is even lower. Trevor Jones of the London Borough of Islington Police Committee Support Unit has calculated that the clear-up rate for burglary on the borough council estates is less than 2.5 per cent.

Detection rates have declined below the level that would have even a marginal deterrent effect: this is the extent of the 'hyper-crisis'.

Changes in the Number of Crimes Cleared Up

Of course, over the period 1973–83 there has been a considerable increase in police resources at every level. It is no
surprise, therefore, to find that the *number* of crimes cleared up
has increased every year, and over the ten-year period, by 48
per cent, in England and Wales. Furthermore, the efficiency of
the police at a national level as measured by the number of
crimes cleared up per officer has also risen by 18 per cent (see
Table 2). It should be noted, however, that the actual number
of crimes cleared up per officer is surprisingly low – 9.5 in a
year – and this would fall to about 7 if we allowed for the
considerable civilian auxiliary back-up in police forces that
has grown over the years. Given the resources poured into
policing and the rise in crime, which presumably provides an
ever-increasing supply of easily cleared up crimes as well as
difficult ones, it is incredible that such a level of efficiency
should not be more closely questioned.

But when we turn to the Metropolitan Police we find an
even more astonishing situation. For the number of crimes
cleared up has risen by only 7 per cent over the ten-year
period in question. Indeed, as can be seen from Figure 3, there
was a period between 1976 and 1981 when there was hardly
any change in the numbers of crimes cleared up despite a 12
per cent increase in manpower. And in some years, such as
1981, there was a decline. And if we turn to the number of
crimes cleared up per police officer every year in London we
arrive at a figure of around 4, a decline of 18 per cent in
efficiency in the decade 1973–83. This gross ineffectiveness
might be seen as a product of the special situation in London
brought about by the demands on the police stemming from
demonstrations, the protection of VIPs and royalty and so on.
But in fact the PSI report found that only 2 per cent of police
time was allocated to such events. It is the scandal of such
figures as these which underscores the extent of the present
crisis in policing.

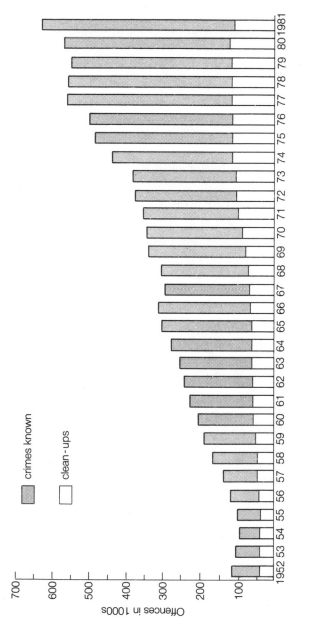

Figure 3 **Numbers of serious offences recorded and cleared up by the Metropolitan Police, 1952–81.**
Source: Newman 1983

Changes in the Number of Crimes not Cleared Up

The changes in the number of crimes which are not cleared up is of more relevance to the public than the number cleared up, because such changes measure the number of times that offenders have committed crimes within the community and got away with it. Justice has not been seen to be done – and the public feel all the more outraged and vulnerable. In terms of public disquiet, it is important to understand how the increase in the quantity of crimes not cleared up makes a qualitative difference to their peace of mind. For if an event is rare, then a low clear-up rate is of little consequence to the majority of people. But if it is frequent – 44 per cent of all homes in Merseyside, for instance, are touched by crime in a year – then a low clear-up rate precipitates alarm. A rare disease which has a 30 per cent rate of cure worries few people, but an epidemic with such a prognosis is a public disaster.

Particularly in the inner cities, where the incidence of crime is exceptionally high, this qualitative leap involves the fear of crime entering into the consciousness of the mass of the people. When one in four houses in working-class areas of Merseyside has been burgled in the last year, then everyone in such areas becomes worried about its likelihood. And crime becomes a potent symbol of everything that has gone wrong in the community, while public attention comes to centre on the police. It is the increase in crime that has brought the police into the focus of public attention. For both their ineffectiveness in dealing with the problem and the 'get tough' measures inflicted on sections of the public in a vain attempt to tackle it, become symbols of a breakdown. The fears for safety in the community and the alienation of the community from the police spring from the same source.

Turning to the figures for crimes not cleared up (see Figure 4), what is striking is the wide disparity occurring since 1975 between the numbers of offences cleared up and those not cleared up. In the earlier years, because the clear-up rate was

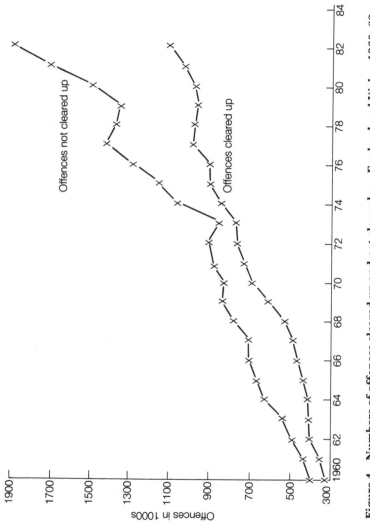

Figure 4 Numbers of offences cleared up and not cleared up, England and Wales, 1960–82.

Source: Annual *Criminal Statistics for England and Wales*

always under 50 per cent at the highest, there was always a divergence, but a numerically small one. But as the total number of crimes grows larger, the gap between solved and unsolved crimes automatically widens. And as there has been since 1975 a 7 per cent drop in the clear-up rate, the chasm becomes all the more significant. With increasingly large numbers of crimes, even a small drop in clearance will produce a numerically high level of crimes not cleared up in relation to those cleared up.

Thus the number of crimes which impact upon the community without even the formality of a legal remedy increases. For every 100 unsolved crimes in 1963 there were 159 in 1973 and 347 in 1983. At the very least they may involve people merely registering their burglary loss at a police station for insurance purposes. At the very worst they will involve a plea for help which goes unanswered. In London one half of crimes of violence against the person and of sexual offences are never cleared up. These are the type of offences which also have a high 'dark figure' of instances unreported because of people's unwillingness to approach the police.

Lastly, it must be noted again that such a qualitative leap in unsolved crimes will be concentrated much more in poor inner-city areas than in the wealthy suburbs. The impact on particularly vulnerable communities will have been much greater than is evident from the gross figures, however shocking these are. The view from the suburbs may be that nothing like a crisis will occur; the view from the inner city is that it has already occurred.

The Cost of Clearing Up Crime

Not only is the rate of crime clear-up extremely low and still decreasing, but the cost is quite staggering. Thus the Home Secretary, replying to a question in the House of Commons (Hansard 9 February 1984), said that in 1982 the cost of clearing up a single crime in the metropolitan counties was

£1,461, while in the Metropolitan Police District it was £5,578. Figures such as these reveal a monstrous inefficiency, particularly when one considers the very broad meaning of 'clear-up'. One might be forgiven for suggesting that a more just use of the money involved would be to simply donate it directly to the victims of crime. After all, 83 per cent of burglaries involve property of value under £500!

In the same parliamentary statement it was suggested by the Secretary of State that there is no basis for comparison between the crime-solving costs for London and for the metropolitan counties because of the high cost of police in London (rates of pay, allowances, accommodation and so on). But as we have seen, this is only part of the story: the high cost of crime cleared up per officer in the Metropolitan Police District has more to do with the fact that the police in London are less than half as effective at clearing up crime as the police forces of the metropolitan counties. The enormous cost of using the police *at their present levels of effectiveness* to clear up crime is seen particularly when we look at calculations of the marginal benefits of, say, a one per cent increase in personnel. The Home Office study *Clearing Up Crime* stated:

On the weight of present evidence there would appear to be little justification for increasing police strength to achieve an increase in clear-up rates. The pay-off to be anticipated from such a move would not be dramatic: unwise though it would be to place too great an emphasis on exact figures, the findings suggest that a one per cent increase in police manpower (which at 1980 prices would cost £12.8 million, NB excluding the cost of civilian staff) would produce less than a one per cent increase in the clear-up rate. (Burrows and Tarling 1982)

In a similar vein, P. E. Crust, in another Home Office Research Unit project, noted in 1975 that the cost of additional manpower required to make significant increases in the clear-up rate would be 'unrealistic' (Home Office 1975).

As we shall discover in more detail in later chapters, this

type of thinking now in vogue at the Home Office has considerable implications for the whole of policing strategy. After all, if increases in police manpower will contribute little to clearing up crime, then it might be better to try other approaches. Also, the discovery that simply 'throwing money' at the problem of crime by increasing spending on manpower will show diminishing returns is beginning to be taken note of by a government determined to reduce government expenditure. Hitherto it has been characteristic of Conservative governments to denounce the throwing of money at social problems, particularly in the inner cities, and to call for 'self-reliance', for the decentralization and privatization of social services and for cuts in social spending, while at the same time steadily increasing police and prison spending. But recently, 'The Home Secretary has told all chief officers and police authorities [circular dated 30 November 1983] that he will not be prepared to approve increases in manpower unless he is satisfied that existing resources are being properly deployed' (Home Office 1984a).

Crisis – What Crisis?

One of the most immediate responses to the crisis in policing is a simple denial of the problem. Thus the crisis becomes hidden under a welter of police public relations handouts. As an example, let us take the interpretations of the crime statistics in London over the last few years. Sir Kenneth Newman, the Commissioner of Police of the metropolis, has been doing his best in recent years to allay any talk of 'crisis'. Sir Kenneth was voted 'communicator of the year' in 1984 by the British Association of Industrial Editors. In presenting the award the president of the association, Mr Michael Montaign, heaped praise on Sir Kenneth: 'By assiduous attention to the information needs of local and national politicians, leaders of local communities and national organisations and representatives of the press and media, he has opened up the Metropolitan Police in a way few have imagined possible. We believe that it is no coincidence that the crime rate in London has started to fall and policing statistics to improve.'

Sir Kenneth's Press release of February 1984 can be taken as an example of his masterly public relations work. The statement, entitled 'Building on Achievement', claimed that in 1983 there was an overall 4 per cent drop in recorded crime, a 5 per cent drop in recorded robbery and other violent theft; a 2 per cent increase in the numbers of crimes cleared up, and a 25 per cent increase in the clear-up rate for robbery and other violent theft. The tide, it might have appeared, was turning. The main public relations message in these figures was that the crisis of policing in London was being resolved and Sir Kenneth was the man who was doing it. The *Sunday Telegraph* echoed these feelings: 'For far too long the criminals have been living in a society where their exploits have begun to assume an aura of invincibility . . . Last week's news should help redress the balance and give the criminals something – if not yet nearly enough – to worry about' (12 February 1984).

What did Sir Kenneth's statistics actually show? In fact, very little had changed. The 4 per cent drop in recorded crime, for example, was presented as if to show that criminals had been deterred by better policing. But once we take into account that in London 94 per cent of serious crimes are reported to the police by the public, then a 4 per cent drop in crime could have just as easily been a 4 per cent drop in public confidence in the police, reflected in fewer crimes being reported. Given a high level of unreported crime, one would expect that an increase in public confidence could easily lead to an increase rather than a decrease in reported crime. The figures, presented by Scotland Yard's public relations department with the inference that good policing is scaring away criminals, are simply untenable. Such claims of progress for 1983 became all the more transparent a year later when the 1984 figures were published, showing that the number of crimes reported to the police had increased by 9 per cent to over 700,000!

Likewise, the astonishing 25 per cent improvement in clear-ups for robbery and other violent theft did not withstand close inspection. The actual clear-up rate for this category of crime was 10 per cent in 1982 and 13 per cent in 1983. So what the 25 per cent increase actually amounted to was a move from a failure rate of 90 per cent to one of 87 – hardly a breakthrough. As to the 2 per cent increase in the numbers of crimes cleared up, the previous year (1982) Sir Kenneth had claimed an increase of 3 per cent, but with a 4.7 per cent increase in police manpower. In 1983, the 2 per cent increase in crimes cleared up was in fact accompanied by a 2 per cent increase in police manpower. At least police efficiency was not declining in 1983, as it had the previous year. But that efficiency remained already low at the absurd figure of 4.2 crimes cleared up per officer. When the 1984 figures were issued, showing the increase in reported crime, one of Scotland Yard's public relations wizards hinted that this setback might be due to the miners' strike (see the police newspaper *The Job* 22 March 1985). But as we have noted, as crime is largely reported by the public to the police, it is difficult to see how having fewer officers around in London would directly affect the rate of public reporting. Indeed, in 1982, two years before Sir Kenneth's 'Building on Achievement' Press release, reported crime had also risen by 9 per cent but with no miners' strike available to explain it away.

However, Sir Kenneth, possibly from a desire to cover all possible contingencies, has also been arguing in a very different direction – namely, that much of the recent growth in crime is of a type which the police cannot in any reasonable sense be expected to control. This view is compatible with the Home Office research on the diminishing-returns effect of increases in police manpower. It is also a view that lies behind the various plans for 'multi-agency' policing (which will be explored in Chapter 6). Increasing public criticism of police efficiency and of their relations with local communities has created an environment in which attempts to secure the cooperation and hence the *responsibility* of agencies other than the police in the fight against crime, become attractive to police managers. Criticisms of low clear-up rates can to some extent be deflected if the public can be persuaded that the police are not the only agency responsible for crime control, and that certain types of crime are almost beyond their capacity to deal with. Thus in his annual report for 1982 Sir Kenneth argued:

One of the most significant features of the growth of crime in recent years has been the expansion of opportunities to commit offences. In practical terms there are more motor cars parked unattended than ever before and the contents of every home now include items which find a ready sale in illegitimate market places. (Newman 1983, p. 6)

It follows, for Sir Kenneth, that the public need to be a lot more realistic about what contribution the police, acting alone, can be expected to make to the fight against crime:

I have already acknowledged that our clear-up rates in the crimes of autocrime and burglary are low. But can the public realistically expect the police acting alone to make an impact on these opportunist and randomly committed crimes? . . . To judge police performance on an overall clear-up rate that is set against the total crime reported, without regard to the nature or solvability of the different types of crime, is misleading. (p. 9)

Thus, without any element of public accountability or public debate, or even debate in the House of Commons, a public official – the Commissioner of Police of the metropolis – has been attempting to bring about fundamental shifts in how the police function is to be legitimately evaluated: not in this instance, it should be noted, by attempting to persuade the public to accept a more authoritarian or 'military' style of policing, but by persuading them to accept a withdrawal of the police as the sole agency responsible for the containment and detection of crime. By erecting 'solvability' as the criterion of whether or not the police should be responsible for the combating of particular types of crime, Sir Kenneth is attempting to pre-empt, in the name of technical–managerial considerations, a fundamental debate about the nature of police–community relations. When is a crime 'solvable' and when not? How 'unsolvable' should a crime be before we admit that the police cannot be regarded as the agency responsible for its detection and containment? How far could the 'solvability' of crimes be increased by *other* methods, such as changes in police organization or, as is advocated in this book, changes in the way police forces operate and in their accountability to local authorities?

In a functioning democracy all these questions need to be aired and debated as widely as possible before the introduction of the sort of innovations that Sir Kenneth has been smuggling into the Met through the 'back door' of organizational and managerial planning. In his annual report for 1983, without any significant public debate, Sir Kenneth had reached the stage of elaborating a fundamentally new conception of the clear-up rate for crime:

If we take the traditional approach to the relationship between clear-up and total recorded crime, it would appear as total crimes cleared up/total recorded crime.

In this presentation, the 'numerator' of cleared-up crimes is subject to a number of variable factors such as the likelihood of solution offered by any particular crime and the policy of a given force for obtaining its clear-ups. The 'denominator' of total recorded crime is likewise subject to influences quite outside police control, such as the will, resources and motivation of a local authority in its approach to crime prevention, any impact on crime made by truancy or by unemployment, or even contrasts between the standard of life purveyed by commercial advertising and the achievements possible in real life.

Seen in this context, it becomes evident that the clear-up rate reflects not only the apparent performance of the police but also of the community as a whole. (Newman 1984, p. 4)

This is quite remarkable. The fact long known to criminologists and thinking people generally, that the *causes* of crime are complex and largely beyond the control of an agency such as the police, is now being recruited to shift the responsibility for *combating* crime from the police to other agencies.

Responses to the Crisis

It is our contention that the various innovations and pro-
nouncements about policing represent attempts to deal with
the crisis. Some of them try to conceal the problem, some to
deflect responsibility away from the police, and others actually
to increase police effectiveness. But all of them, for very good
reasons – and to the chagrin of their originators – are
counterproductive. We have seen that any claim that the
situation is under control and the crisis over is belied by the
cruel litany of the annual crime statistics. But there are more
sophisticated rhetorical responses to the crisis. It is possible to
deny that crime is really a problem. It is even possible to
suggest that policing, by its very nature, can only achieve
limited gains in the fight against crime. These arguments will
be examined in later chapters.

We shall then proceed to look at some of the more practical
and institutional innovations intended to deal with the crisis.
Not all of these measures are of the same type. On the one
hand are what might be called 'hard' measures. Among these
could be included the increasing reliance on computers and
criminal intelligence, and many of the measures included in
the Police and Criminal Evidence Act 1984, which codified
and increased police powers relating to arrest, the detention of
suspects and powers of stop and search. On the other hand,
there have developed a number of 'soft' measures designed to
increase police contact with the community, and initiatives
designed to mobilize the community as a source of information
about crime, as well as to mobilize other agencies, together
with the public itself, into taking on an increased share of the
tasks of crime control. Inter-agency cooperation between the
police, the social services, housing and education departments
of local government, and the establishment of Neighbourhood
Watch and community liaison panels, are some of the more
important innovations.

In the following chapters we shall look at some of these
measures, together with their accompanying problems. We

shall argue that these measures will not work, that they will not solve the crisis of rising crime and declining clear-up rates. In the concluding chapters we contend that only an informed socialist policy, involving the restructuring of the relations between police, local community and local government, is likely ever to make our cities tolerable places for working-class people to live in.

2

Vicious Circles:
Increasing Alienation

The mass media present stereotypical depictions not only of crime but also of policing. It would perhaps make rather untidy television drama if the denouement usually showed the culprit getting away once again, but this would be closer to the truth. Similarly, the staple of detective fiction, from Inspector Poirot to Starsky and Hutch, of the painstaking, dramatic and 'scientific' investigation leading always to the detection of the offender, is largely a myth. Investigative policing, like investigative journalism, is a rare event. The typical crime is reported to the police by the public and is solved through public cooperation. As we have noted, it is certainly not usually discovered by the police, with the exception of minor crimes involved in public disorder.

Over 90 per cent of serious crime in Britain is reported by the public to the police; this rises to over 95 per cent in city areas. The information usually consists of the facts of the crime and a very good indication of who did it. This is especially true of crimes of violence, where the victim more often than not knows exactly who committed the crime, given that such crimes are usually carried out by relatives and close friends. But even the detection of burglary depends overwhelmingly upon public witnessing.

Thus the flow of information from the public to the police is crucial. Where the public support the police, they will maintain the flow. When that flow of information dries up, successful policing becomes tremendously difficult. There can be two reasons for the drying-up of the information. First, there may be no information available; second, the relevant public may not be willing to impart it to the police. A clear example of both these circumstances prevailing was the case of the Yorkshire Ripper investigation. Although there was, undoubtedly, a good deal of inefficiency in police inquiries, criticism which centres on the inability of the police to solve the crime despite the huge resources available misses the mark, and is based on a fundamental misconception as to the nature of effective policing. The actual problem was twofold. First, random killing, where the murderer does not previously know the victim, where there are no witnesses and where the victim is dead, is notoriously difficult to solve. From Jack the Ripper to the Boston Strangler, such serial murders have been particularly impenetrable wherever they have occurred. It is only those people who have a media-inflated conception of the effectiveness of forensic science and 'rational' police work who could believe otherwise. Second, although there was a considerable consensus amongst the public in support of the police task, the key group, the *relevant* public which might have had some information to convey, were reluctant to cooperate with them. Thus Michael Nicholson writes: 'We have . . . established that one advantage of selecting prostitutes as victims is the smokescreen which surrounds a police investigation of this nature and invariably a great reluctance of witnesses to come forward. This can only help the killer' (Nicholson 1979, p. 161). Many prostitutes were unwilling to cooperate because of fear of the police, based on past experience. Even more unwilling to come forward were the clients. Where the police do not have much information from the public concerning the likely suspects for a crime, they must suspect whole categories of people indiscriminately. Thus in the Yorkshire Ripper case the police had to suspect all men who might have visited prostitutes.

The same principle operates with regard to any section of

the community whose relations with the police are at a low ebb. In areas like Brixton, in inner London, where relations between the police and the black community have deteriorated seriously, the police suspect all young black males of being involved in street crime. It should not be thought that this necessarily reflects some failing on the part of the public to maintain good relations with the police. The bad relations and the reluctance of the relevant sections of the public to yield up information may be a result of past police action. Indeed, this decline in the flow of information takes the form of a vicious circle. Where information flow declines, instead of reacting to public information the police act proactively according to their own hunches and generalizations. In the vast majority of crimes this is a procedure doomed to failure. For crimes are typically committed sporadically, not by committed professional criminals but by amateurs, and by a tiny minority of any category of people at any one time. So if police take to stopping and searching 'likely' candidates in the street for a particular offence, they are almost certain to stop a vast number of innocent people. Precisely because of this innocence, anger with and alienation from the police is the very likely result. It is important to realize that such a vicious circle has a dynamic of its own: it is not simply the result of the police being bloody-minded in a vacuum, nor is it simply the response of an overworked police force to rising crime rates.

The general drift of this vicious circle is away from what can be called consensus policing and towards what can be called military policing. Consensus policing involves the notion of police working to control crime with the bulk of the community supporting, or at least tolerating, their activities. The police officer is in and with the community. His or her knowledge of crime is extensive, and information is readily forthcoming from the community. Such an ideal state of affairs has probably been approximated only in rural communities. In working-class areas of the city there has always been a degree of distance between police and community. If consensus policing is one end of a continuum, it is away from this end and towards its polar opposite that urban policing in this country is moving.

The old notion of consensus policing rested on certain assumptions about the social structure of the city – assumptions that are now crumbling. It presupposed a stable working-class community opposed to crime (most working-class crime is directed against working-class people). The police would catch and/or deter individual offenders on the assumption that the community would tolerate police activity and act as a source of information, making such activity possible. True, policing also functioned as an instrument of naked class politics, as on the picket line. But this was an episodic activity, not part of the day-to-day process of urban policing.

With rising long-term unemployment in the inner city, the whole basis for this type of policing begins to crumble. Crime rates rise rapidly, and the police begin to adopt high-profile strategies – like stop and search – aimed less at identifiable offenders located with the aid of information obtained from the community, and more against the community itself or, at least, the young. The distinction between offender and non-offender begins to blur, and the situation approaches one in which any young person is as likely as any other to be caught in the net of stop and search or by other forms of aggressive policing, quite irrespective of his or her actions. Once this happens, then two further developments begin to crystalize.

First, the community becomes alienated from the police and begins to dry up as a source of information and cooperation. This makes it harder for the police to carry out the older strategies of consensus policing, tracking down individuals. To get any information at all the police have increasingly to engage in 'dragnet'-type operations, which serve to further alienate the community at large and have a low productivity. The 'Swamp 81' operation conducted by the Metropolitan Police in Brixton, which preceded the rioting in that area in summer 1981, serves as a tailor-made example of how to antagonize the greatest possible number of people while at the same time achieving minimum efficiency in the control of a particular type of crime – in this case, street robbery.

The instructions to police officers for Swamp 81 stated that 'The purpose of this operation [was] to flood [with police] identified areas on 'L' district [Lambeth] to detect and arrest burglars and robbers.' But as it was unlikely that a mugging, for example, was going to take place directly under the noses of police officers, the operation involved the random stopping of suspect youths. This operation not only alienated the local community, but it was doomed to failure as a crime prevention exercise. The typical footpad or street thief is hardly likely to be carrying a snatched bag with him; stolen money is undetectable; and weapons are used only in a minority of cases. Such police operations therefore make little sense as part of an attempt to locate particular offenders and apprehend them. They may yield some information, but only by chance. They can, however, be seen to make sense as a strategy of general deterrence: a show of force to remind the community that the police can control the streets.

The second effect of such tactics might be called the 'mobilization of bystanders'. For, once the trust between police and community that characterizes consensus policing has broken down, and the police have blurred the distinction between innocent and offender, then the community begins to do likewise and comes to see any attempt at an arrest by police officers as a symbolic attack on the community itself. This deterioration in police–community relations leads to a drying-up of information flowing from public to police, which in turn forms the background for the further development of 'military', or hard, policing. This then alienates the community even further, and again a vicious circle is set up. The chain of events is illustrated in Figure 5 (for a fuller discussion see Lea and Young 1984).

The move from consensus towards military-style policing involves a large number of concomitant changes. Table 3 lists some of the contrasting components of the two styles, and we shall be referring back to these throughout the book.

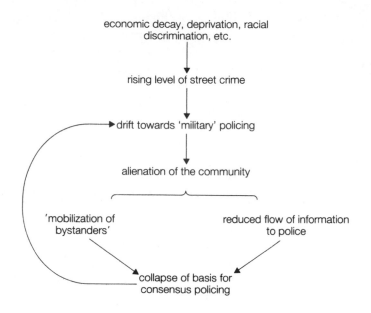

economic decay, deprivation, racial
discrimination, etc.

rising level of street crime

drift towards 'military' policing

alienation of the community

'mobilization of
bystanders'

reduced flow of information
to police

collapse of basis for
consensus policing

Figure 5   The vicious circle of the collapse of consensus policing.

The Marginalized Police Officer

The process of marginalization is two-way – the community is marginalized from the police and the police are increasingly distanced from the public. It is important to bear in mind that the residential segregation of the police, together with their class background and ethnic composition, facilitates such a process. This is manifested first of all in police attitudes, as one police officer interviewed in the PSI report illustrated: 'We only deal with 5 to 10 per cent of the population, that's the slag. Ordinary people don't need to have anything to do with us . . .' (PSI 1983, vol. 4, p. 180).

The PSI researchers David Smith and Jeremy Gray note how this distinction between 'slag' and 'ordinary people' gives rise to the notion that the police need not stick to the same

Table 3 Two types of policing: consensus and military

Subject	Consensus policing	Military policing
The public	supports the police	fears/is in conflict with the police
Information from the public	large amount, relevant to crime detection and specific	small amount, low-grade and general
Mode of gathering information	public-initiated, low use of police surveillance technology	police-initiated, extensive use of surveillance technology
Police profile	low profile, integrated with community, police officers as citizens	high profile, police as outsiders, marginalized, use of force and special militarized units
Targeting by police	of specific offenders	of social groups/stereotyped populations
Style of police intervention	individual, consensual, reactive	generalized, coercive, proactive
Ideal typical example	English village	Northern Ireland

rules in dealing with both populations. You are more suspicious of the 'slags', and you take their complaints less
seriously. In part, they note, this relates to the class origins of
most police officers. Predominantly from upper-working-class
or lower-middle-class backgrounds, they distinguish strongly –
and are preoccupied with the distinction – between the
'respectable' and the 'non-respectable' working class. Thus
even before the process of marginalization of the community
from the police which we have described as a vicious circle,
there is *already* a well documented distance between the police
and the poeple who are the object of policing (see Young
1971). What has been less often noted, however, is that this
process of segregation is highly structured. Thus if we compare
inner-city Granby with suburban Ainsdale in Merseyside, we
find distinct differences in the extent to which members of the
public are personally acquainted with police officers (see
Table 4).

The major point here is that police officers are segregated
from high crime rate areas – they have little social contact
with the people most likely to be offenders or victims. They
are not at all segregated from middle-class and respectable
working-class people. This reflects both their own social
origins and their ambitions for upward mobility. Of course, at
the beginning of their careers some young police officers may
well live in the inner city but, for most, after a few years, the
move to the suburbs, the working-class dream of upward
mobility, is enacted. And it is not only in terms of class that the
police are selected from a narrow range of the population: it is
also true in terms of ethnic background. Thus in London the
PSI found that 99.5 per cent of the police are white and that
racial prejudice is endemic. We can thus see the police officer,
driving in from the suburbs to police an inner-city population
from whom he is alienated by background and whom he
considers inferior, as the starting-point for the further alienation of the police from the public.

Table 4   Contact with police officers known to respondents by name in Ainsdale and in Granby (%)

Respondents knowing police officers by name in:	How known			
	Close friend or relative	Neighbour	Through work	Seen regularly on duty
Ainsdale 51	21	30	11	10
Granby 24	7	8	4	10

Source: Kinsey, 1984

The Alienation of the Public from the Police

What evidence do we have for our hypothesis of the marginalization and alienation from the police of those sections of the community most vulnerable to crime, and of the result of policing as the antagonism (and frequent mobilization against the police) of innocent bystanders? The prevalence of the unequal treatment of young people and of ethnic minorities is more widely recognized by the general public than is often realized. According to the *Merseyside Crime Survey*, in the working-class areas of Merseyside a third of respondents believe that the police do not treat all groups of people equally, and they overwhelmingly single out young people and blacks as receiving unfair treatment. It is only in those areas with little crime that a belief in the impartiality of the police is held by more than 70 per cent of respondents.

Similarly, the PSI report on the Metropolitan Police found that 29 per cent of Londoners thought that the police treated particular groups unfairly, almost all pinpointing ethnic minorities and young people. Furthermore, the researchers found that 62 per cent of West Indians thought that there was unfair treatment, as did over 40 per cent of young people under 24. When we combine these two categories – young West Indians and the under-24s – one is left with a figure of 68 per cent (PSI 1983, vol. 1, pp. 242–6). Such a widespread disbelief in police fairness, doubling in the case of certain critical groups, indicates a collective disquiet based on experience and only too real in its consequences.

It might of course be argued that in terms of official statistics at least, young people have a high crime rate, and so their belief in police unfairness reflects simply an objection to police interference in their criminal activities. Such an argument shows a fundamental misunderstanding of the nature of crime, and of youth crime in particular. Serious offences involve only a minority of the population at any one time. The involvement of young people in crime is overwhelmingly minor and sporadic. Kids drift in and out of delinquency; they are infrequently heavily committed to criminal careers. The trouble starts when the police, instead of acting on specific information, stereotype a whole category of people as potentially guilty, and engage in indiscriminate acts of stop and search. Such a situation is a direct result of the spiral of lessening information and public cooperation that we have detailed.

Thus it is precisely those groups of people who for reasons of social structure – for example, high unemployment, marginalization and deprivation – are most socially and economically deprived, who are also the most critical of the police and the judicial system. In the absence of any political method of redressing this balance, the potential for crime is enormous. For, as was pointed out in *What Is To Be Done About Law and Order?* (Lea and Young 1984), police illegality is a potent source of crime:

It cannot be overemphasised the extent to which bad policing leads to an increase in crime. Illegalities by the police, of a blatantly prejudiced character such as in racist attacks, serve to break the bond with legality. In the case of black youth, for instance, not only are they economically discarded but then their political marginalization and lack of muscle are brought home to them by illegal treatment at the hands of the police . . .

In a situation where the police become marginalized from a community, not only do they commit more illegalities and thus generate discontent with the law, and hence crime, but they receive less information, thus facilitating the successful commission of crime in terms of chances of being detected. Thus the process depicted in the accompanying diagram occurs. Thus police marginalization

contributes greatly to the feelings of deprivation which cause crime and the circumstances which make crime all the more possible. (pp. 61–2)

Further remarkable evidence of what we termed above the 'bystander effect' is the finding by the PSI report that the highest correlate of being stopped and searched in the streets of London is the liklehihood not of being an offender but of being a victim of crime:

There is an even stronger relationship between being a victim and being stopped by police (and therefore suspected of an offence). It is people who are repeatedly stopped who are most likely to be also victims. For example, among people who have been stopped by the police twice or more in the past year, 59 per cent have also been victims of some offence, and the mean number of cases of victimization is 1.21; whereas among people who have not come to police notice for any offence or suspected offence, only 18 per cent have been victims, and the mean number of incidents of victimization is 0.30. (PSI 1983, vol. 1, p. 314)

We have pointed to two interrelated vicious circles involving both the police and vulnerable sections of the population. On one level a largely innocent population is cast by the police in a criminal role, with a consequent drying up of the flow of information about crime. On the other level, some small proportion of that already economically deprived section of the population is precipitated into a further increase in crime. We have created in this country a criminal justice system which alienates precisely that section of the population which would otherwise be the main source of information about crime and the public bedrock of successful policing. Further, we allow this apparatus to impinge unjustly on those people most at risk of becoming criminal. A more successful recipe for disaster could not be imagined.

Some Objections to our Thesis

It might be argued that there has been a falling off in information to the police not because of police behaviour so much as community disintegration, not so much because the public is alienated from the police but because there is less knowledge about crime for the community to impart. Second, it might be argued that repeated public opinion polls reveal a widespread support for the police which scarcely indicates a collapse of consensus policing. In this way the crisis of policing could be seen simply as a product of the disintegration of community in the inner city: in those areas where there is highest community breakdown, there is both a high rate of crime and less available information about it. If this were so the problem would be less that of information flow than of less information available.

In fact, however, the *Merseyside Crime Survey* provides important corroboration of our argument and a falsification of the 'lack of information in the first place' argument. It was found that there was considerably higher knowledge of crime in the poorer areas than in the richer ones. Comparing, for example, Granby with Ainsdale, we found dramatic differences in the direct witnessing of crimes, as shown in Table 5.

Table 5   Individuals who witnessed offences in the previous five years in Granby and in Ainsdale (%)

Offence	Granby	Ainsdale	Ratio Granby: Ainsdale
Vandalism	41	17	2.4:1
Indecent exposure	7	4	1.8:1
Theft from motor car	21	4	5.3:1
Serious fighting	29	14	2.1:1

Source: Kinsey, 1984

Even in absolute terms, 1 in 5 Granby residents having witnessed a theft from a motor car is an extremely high figure. What is different, however, is the willingness to cooperate with the police. In Table 6 we compare the two areas on public willingness to assist the police in three hypothetical crime situations.

Table 6   Willingness of individuals to cooperate with the police in Granby and in Ainsdale (%)

Incident		Prepared to tell police	Prepared to identify offender	Prepared to give evidence in court
Bus shelter vandalism	Granby	66	59	54
	Ainsdale	97	91	86
Mugging	Granby	88	80	72
	Ainsdale	100	98	93
Accident	Granby	97	–	94
	Ainsdale	98	–	95

Source: Kinsey, 1984

Here the Merseyside survey echoes the results found in London by the PSI report but, very usefully for our purposes, specifies variation between areas rather than differences between categories of the population. Note first of all that in the case of a road accident, where there is no criminal offence, nearly everyone in both areas is very willing to cooperate. But in the case of criminal offences, there are considerable differences between the two areas.

It might be argued that what is faulty is not the relationship between the police and the public but relations within the community itself. For example, there might be a general indifference in high crime areas, but in more 'respectable' areas people may perceive it as their business, when observing crime, to report it to the police. But in fact the reverse is the case. In all areas the major reason why people would not report, say, a mugging to the police is fear of reprisal, followed by that of not wanting to get involved with the police. Thus in the Merseyside area as a whole, the reasons given for not wanting to help the police in regard to mugging were: fear of reprisal – 55 per cent; not wanting to get involved with the police – 12 per cent; 'It's not my business' – 11 per cent; and other reasons – 22 per cent.

The first two reasons relate to confidence in the police: confidence that they will protect you and a conviction that they will not harass you. The third reason is a measure of indifference, small by comparison with the other two. However, this public indifference varies by area: it is low in Granby (8 per cent) and high in Ainsdale (20 per cent), and the same pattern is true of poor working-class areas as a whole – 7 per cent in Northwood compared with 23 per cent in respectable, suburban Haydock, for example.

We have defined the notion of information flow and its relationship to successful policing. Where there is least crime and least knowledge of crime, there is the most willingness to help the police; where there is most crime and knowledge, there is least willingness to cooperate. And these two principles apply to very different areas of a city, and not simply to ethnically mixed inner-city Granby compared with middle-class suburban Ainsdale. These are extremes, poles apart, but as we have seen in other indices of attitudes to and experience of crime and the police, there is a definite grouping of areas. Inner-city Granby and Birkenhead are similar to the poor outer-city council estates of Northwood; surburban, respectable working-class Haydock is like middle-class Ainsdale. Poor areas and poor people have the greatest need of effective policing, yet are the most alienated from the police force which is supposed to serve them.

The differential rates of victimization of the poor and the wealthy corespond to two different types of policing. The move to hard or military-style policing does not proceed evenly across the country, nor has consensus policing disappeared. Consensus policing serves quite well in the low-crime, affluent areas of the country where there is substantial support for the police and least need for them. The move towards military-style, hard policing is seen most clearly in the inner-city areas, where it augments the growing alienation and exacerbates the community's problems of crime control.

The Information Crisis: The Police Response

Despite the smokescreen of public relations, the various recent innovations in policing centre predominantly on tackling the crisis in crime control, and display an increasing awareness of the problems of public alienation from the police and the lack of information flow. In later chapters we shall look at some of these developments in detail, but for the moment let us note the general principles involved. What we are suggesting is that, however imperfectly, the police establishment comprehends the crisis facing them, and their responses are understandable as an attempt to deal with it. The innovations and developments in policing strategy are not part of a swing to the 'strong state' in some automatic fashion *unrelated* to the pressing problems of crime control. Equally, such innovations are not to be understood as the pragmatic adoption of new techniques – computerization, for example – simply because they have become available.

In arguing that the key to recent developments in policing is the attempt to come to grips with the crisis in crime control, we do not deny the role of industrial disputes, political demonstrations and terrorism in shaping the modern police force. We would simply point out that the major, day-to-day, task of policing, and the job most highly regarded in police culture, is that of crime control. It is in this area that there is a *continual* pressing crisis. This cannot be over emphasized, for there has been in recent years a host of books on policing which move from one industrial dispute to another, from riot to demonstration, from public order among barrow boys to the social control of working-class street culture, all of which fail to mention crime.

A sense of perspective can be gained by looking at the proportion of time that the police spend on political events. The PSI report makes this point on the subject of policing London: 'The proportion of time spent at 'special events' is low (2 per cent). This shows that the public order responsibilities of the police, which are much greater in London than elsewhere in the country, are not a very significant reason for the diversion of resources from patrolling' (PSI 1983, vol. 3, p. 40). Even at the height of the miners' strike in 1984, the percentage of time spent on policing the strike was small. In Merseyside it was 4.5 per cent and this was totally made up of overtime. Although innovations in policing resulting from the policing of political conflicts may have an effect on crime-control policing, they are not adopted unchanged. What is insidious is the argument that the policing of overtly political conflicts is, in fact, identical with normal policing, and that even crime may be seen as a proto-revolutionary activity against the property relations of capitalist society.

Thus, for example, Tony Bunyan in his influential book *The Political Police in Britain* writes of the history of the police:

Policing was (and still is) concerned with two areas – public order and crime. The maintenance of public order was essential to frustrate the nationwide struggles by the new working class . . . Crime on the other hand largely concerned individual acts against the propertied classes, such as stealing from factories, pickpocketing, assault and robbery and burglary . . . The ruling class sought security for their property (home and factory) and in their everyday lives. (1976, pp. 61–2)

Crime, as a casual perusal of the criminal statistics will show, is not a series of political acts conducted against the bourgeoisie by the working class. If this were so then the rapid rise in the crime rate would have some effects in the form of a fundamental transfer of wealth. As we have noted, crime is predominantly reported to the police by people of working- and middle-class backgrounds, and committed against them by people from similar backgrounds. The problem with views such as Bunyan's is that not only are they grossly inaccurate, but they are also politically dangerous. If we believe that the *predominant* role of the police is now the political control of radical political movements (and that crime is somehow part of this radical politics), then we shall be insensitive to and unprepared to recognize those changes in the role of the police that governments of the authoritarian right, under conditions of mounting political conflict, attempt to bring about under the guise of 'preserving law and order'.

We argue that up to the present time the overwhelming problem facing the police, from their own perspective, has been that of increasing their efficiency in crime control and of improving their public image, all without giving way to the growing demands for increased public accountability. As we have seen, three types of strategy have been evolved to meet these problems: the denial or playing down of crime as a problem, the increase in the flow of public information to the police, and the hiving off of some crime control tasks to other agencies.

1   The playing down of crime as a problem. The argument is commonly put forward that fear of crime is more of a problem than crime itself. It is asserted that people have an exaggerated notion of crime and do not realize that most crime is of a minor and of a property nature. Furthermore, fear of crime, by forcing people off the streets, particularly at night, can create a self-fulfilling prophecy, resulting in a weakening of informal neighbourhood social control and a consequent rise in crime. Institutions such as beat policing and community policing can, it is argued, decrease the fear of crime, even though they may have no or little effect on the actual crime rate. *The British Crime Survey* and similar victimization surveys are used to argue that the risks of crime are, in most instances, minimal.

2   Measures to increase the flow of information. If the police can increase the flow of information to them from the public, then their problem is to a large extent solved. Measures to increase information flow can be divided into 'hard' and 'soft'. Hard measures include strengthening the powers of traditional police methods. For example, the Police and Criminal Evidence Act 1984 increases the powers of stop and search and detention of suspects. This, it is hoped, will provide the police with a greater facility for gathering information from the public. It is also hoped that the detention of suspects and extended interrogation will increase the number of crimes 'taken into consideration', and thus help to increase the clear-up rate.

Also among hard measures can be included the use of more advanced computer systems, which allow information to be stored and retrieved in a sophisticated way, analysed, and rapidly made ready for use. By this means it is hoped to 'target' likely criminals more accurately and reduce the possibility of false accusations or arrest. Additionally, computerization will allow the more rapid collation of police-gathered information, thus helping to sidestep the need for reliance on information voluntarily supplied by the public.

If hard policing attempts to get round the information crisis by developing sources of information-gathering not dependent on public cooperation or by giving police more power to prise information out of the public, 'soft' measures aim to bring the public into closer relationship with the police and, together with other agencies in social work and local government, to take a more active role in controlling crime as well as in feeding information to the police. Thus Neighbourhood Watch schemes involve the public channelling information to the police through liaison with local beat constables, and at the same time act as a deterrent to crime by virtue of their very existence. Likewise, new initiatives in 'multi-agency' policing involve a wide spectrum of agencies, under police leadership, cooperating to work out effective strategies of crime prevention.

These measures will not work, even though some of them contain elements which, in an environment of democratic police accountability, could have useful roles to play. More particularly, we shall argue, they do not form a coherent strategy. The hard and soft measures tend to pull in different directions.

3   *Hiving off and reprioritization.* Although all crimes are import-ant, those which are really serious and less frequent can be differentiated from those which are less serious and more frequent. Thus Sir Kenneth Newman classified burglary and auto-crime (theft of motor vehicles) as 'secondary' crime which the public cannot expect the police to deal with alone. This concern to redefine some crime as 'secondary' is to be understood in the context of Newman's desire to play down the clear-up rate as a reliable index of police efficiency. He argues that clear-up rates are heavily weighted by burglary and auto-crime statistics, crimes which are largely unsolvable but constitute a large part of the total. If they can be removed, then clear-up rates for 'real' police work such as murder and armed robbery look much better. Home security, property-marking and other ways of 'hardening the target' for the burglar are thus seen as useful ways in which the public can take over some of the tasks of crime prevention. Neighbour-hood Watch schemes also fulfil such a role.

In the following chapters we shall discuss the extent to which these strategies will be able to solve the crisis in crime control. Our conclusion will be that they cannot, and that only a reorganization of policing and its aims and methods, coupled with the democratic control of police forces by local government, will offer a way forward in the fight against crime.

3

The Politics of Policing:
A Strange Consensus of
Left and Right

On the basis of the evidence that we have reviewed so far, it would seem to be a legitimate conclusion that crime is a growing social problem. However, a notable feature of recent years has been the growth of a body of 'informed' opinion over a wide range of the political spectrum, which takes the view that crime is not really much of a problem at all. It is, for example, common ground between the Home Office, certain senior police officers and some left-wing writers that the seriousness of crime is exaggerated.

A good recent example of this thinking is provided by two writers on the left, Mick Ryan and Joe Sim, in an article in *The Abolitionist* (Ryan and Sim 1984). *The Abolitionist* is an excellent journal that presents the case from the left for radical alternatives to the existing prison system. The article in question, entitled 'Decoding Leon Brittan', is an attack on the Home Secretary's address to the Conservative Party Conference in 1983 and on the Howard League for Penal Reform which advocates, among other things, far stronger prison sentences for violence. Ryan and Sim argue, correctly in our opinion, that tougher sentencing is largely ineffective as a deterrent. They also argue, and here we part company with them, that violence is a comparatively rare event anyway. In other words, not only had the Home Secretary proposed the wrong remedy for the problem, but there wasn't much of a problem to start with.

They begin by noting that the overwhelming majority of crimes are of a 'petty property nature'. They quote approvingly someone of a rather different political persuasion from themselves, Sir Robert Mark, a former Commissioner of Police of the Metropolis, who wrote in his autobiography:

Take crime, for example. Always good for a headline or for the politician whipping up emotional support. It monopolises much of the television screen, the movies, the world of what laughingly passes for literature. It is an endless source of argument and debate. Of course to the victim of crime the word has real and often distressing meaning. But seen objectively against the background and problems of 50 million people it is not even amongst the more serious of our difficulties. Of the 2,100,000 crimes recorded in 1976 only 5 per cent would be classified as violent, and of these a very high proportion were cleared up. (Mark 1978, p. 241)

Ryan and Sim go on to argue that this pattern, this lack of seriousness of crime, has continued. They substantiate this by quoting from the Home Office's *Criminal Statistics for England and Wales*:

The latest Criminal Statistics for England and Wales 1982 reveal a similar picture. The Home Office authors note that the vast majority (over 95 per cent) of the 3.25 million notifiable offences recorded by the police during the year were offences against property, and many of these were comparatively trivial. (Ryan and Sim 1984, p. 4)

They quote from the report:

A large proportion of recorded offences of theft and burglary involved the stealing of relatively small amounts of property. For recorded offences of theft, other than the taking of motor vehicles, about three-quarters involved stolen property valued at under £100. In about a quarter of recorded offences of burglary nothing was stolen and about a further two-fifths involved property valued at under £100. The distribution of value of property stolen in offences recorded in 1982 was similar to that in earlier years, when inflation is taken into account. (Home Office 1982, p. 32)

and comment:

With regard to assaults the statistics indicate that as in previous years under 5 per cent of all offences recorded by the police were offences against the person. There were, in fact, about 109,000 offences of violence against the person recorded in 1982 of which the great majority (102,000) were of a less serious kind, i.e., broadly, offences of wounding and assault not endangering life. The number of recorded offences of robbery at 23,000 and of sexual offences (20,000) were each under .75 per cent of the total number of offences recorded. (Ryan and Sim, p. 4)

That these quotations from Sir Robert Mark and the Home Office were cited without any criticism by two left-wing writers illustrates the consensus which exists across the political spectrum.

The Home Office has argued this position in its own sophisticated way. Their own Home Office Research Unit in its submission to the 1983 interdepartmental group report on crime notes that:

Whatever the increases, the risks of falling victim to serious crime are still low in England and Wales . . . The average householder is likely to be burgled once in 30 years, while the average car owner will have his vehicle taken once in 50 years . . . Only 5 per cent of crimes recorded by the police involve confrontations, and contrary to popular belief the victims are most likely to be young males not the elderly. The remaining crimes are against property and the vast majority involve small sums. Two thirds of burglaries involve losses under £100. (Home Office 1983a, p. 1)

So what is the essence of this remarkable consensus? It is basically that violent crime is a rarity and that most violence is not really serious; property crime is more common but it is of a minor nature; and violence is not a serious problem when considered alongside other problems faced by the population.

In *What Is To Be Done About Law And Order?* (Lea and Young 1984) it was argued that such a position underestimates the problem of crime by generalizing from average risk rates for the total population, thereby ignoring the risks faced by specific groups. We can now separate out four main, and interrelated, factors in this process, which we shall call underestimation, focusing, compounding and differential vulnerability. We shall look at each of these in turn and focus specifically on the problem of violence, since it might be argued that even though 'run of the mill' property crime does indeed focus on certain sections of the population, violence is still even here a rarity, because it involves such a small number of offences.

Underestimation

Underestimation refers to unreported crime, those crimes unknown to the police and unrecorded in the official crime statistics. There are good reasons for believing that crimes of violence are less likely to be reported to the police than property offences. If people believe the police are inefficient, then it will not be considered worthwhile to report offences. Or particular groups, such as ethnic minorities, may fear that any approach to the police, even to report an offence, may result in harassment by the police or reprisals from the offender. The police may not record the complaint, seeing it as not serious enough. One can assume, though, that property offences will be more often reported. Insurance registration rather than any hope of police action must be a significant factor.

As we have seen in the previous chapter, the police are more likely to record those crimes that fit their stereotypes of 'real' crime. The determinants are the type of crime and who it is committed against. 'Rubbish' crimes, as they are disparagingly called by the police, refer to crimes such as male violence against women in the home, while the 'good arrest' concerns a successful criminal involved in a property crime (PSI 1983, vol. 4). For the distinctions that can be made between what are regarded from the police perspective as 'good' crimes and 'bad' crimes, see Table 7.

Table 7 *'Good' crimes and 'bad' crimes*

	'Good'	'Bad'
Victim	middle- or respectable working-class, white, male	lower-class, ethnic minority, female
Offender	professional criminal	amateur
Occurrence	public	domestic
Relations between offender and victim	stranger	friends, relatives, lovers
Type of crime	property	violence
Detection	police-detected	public-reported

It becomes clear that certain sorts of crime are systematically underestimated: for instance, domestic violence and inter-personal violence between lower-working-class people. But, of course, these are also two of the major forms of violence in our society. For such reasons criminal victimization surveys, which ask the public themselves what crimes have been committed against them during a given period, are an obvious advance on the official crime statistics, with which they can be compared to calculate the proportion of crimes actually reported to the police. Thus *The British Crime Survey* (Hough and Mayhew 1983) found that the following percentages of various offences were reported:

	%
Theft of motor vehicle	95
Burglary	66
Bicycle theft	64
Robbery	47
Wounding	39
Sexual assault	28

Our attention is immediately drawn to the extremely low rate of reporting for sexual assault – only 28 per cent. A similar study conducted by the Scottish Office in 1983 found that only 7 per cent of sexual assaults were reported to the police. But even these figures are most likely based on an underestimation. Although criminal victimization studies have some advantages over the official crime statistics, they also have obvious limitations. People may be unwilling to reveal to an interviewer the extent or nature of their victimization, because of embarassment or fear. This is particularly likely in the case of violence against women. The authors of *The British Crime Survey* commented as follows:

Something should be said about offences against women – 'wife-battering', indecent assault, attempted rape and rape. A small minority (10 per cent) of assault victims were women who had been assaulted by their present or previous husbands or boyfriends. This proportion may well be an underestimate. Many such victims may be unprepared to report incidents of this nature to an interviewer; they may not feel that assaults of this sort fall within the survey's scope, or they may feel embarassment or shame. Indeed, their assailant may be in the same room at the time of interview.

The survey showed a very low rate for rape and other sexual offences. In fact, only one rape was uncovered and that was an attempt. This reflected the rarity of sexual attacks by complete strangers. However, leaving aside definitional problems and any sampling error, some under-counting of such offences committed by non-strangers may have arisen from respondents' reluctance to relive a painful or embarrassing experience for the benefit of a survey interviewer. (Hough and Mayhew 1983, p. 21)

There are two directions in which research can move to try and uncover the real extent of violence against women. One is to try and get at the rate of physical assault indirectly. The most accurate statistics concerning violent crime are probably the homicide statistics. Dead bodies are easier to count and harder to conceal than forms of violence that do not result in death, and with the exception of children and old people they may be taken as tolerably accurate. Homicide in Britain (using the 1982 statistics) is typically committed by a man (91 per cent) against a woman (43 per cent) or another man (48 per cent). Most women victims are killed by their husbands, lovers or ex-lovers, or other members of their family (71 per cent). One could reasonably expect that the ratio of men to women murdered would be reflected in the rate of men to women physically assaulted. Indeed, there are good arguments to suggest that women are more vulnerable to physical assault (notably in the home) than men. Be that as it may, one could expect the ratio of physical assaults to murders to be at least equal for women to that of men. Thus if women are as rarely assaulted as even the victimization survey statistics show by comparison to men, then we would expect many more men to be murdered than women. But this is not so. Women overall suffer a murder rate only a little less than that for men. The ratio is 1:1.2. In the age group 30–49 it is almost the same for both men and women.

A second method is to refine the techniques of victimization surveys. A group of women researchers at Bradford University, finding *The British Crime Survey* results astonishing, found, through the simple use of a female interviewer in a sympathetic interview situation, three rapes and one attempted rape together with a large number of sexual assaults over a twelve-month period in a sample of 129 women in Leeds (Hanmer and Saunders 1984). In a London inquiry into rape and sexual assault, using what was, admittedly, an unorthodox research methodology, 17 per cent in a survey of over 1,000 women reported that they had been raped, and 31 per cent that they had been sexually assaulted (Hall 1985). Of course, such figures are not directly comparable to those of such works as *The British Crime Survey*, because there was no restriction on the time period over which the incidents counted in the survey might have occurred. In other words, the object was to find out whether women had ever experienced violence rather than whether they had experienced it over the previous twelve months. Nevertheless, this survey is an important contribution, particularly in respect of the percentage of incidents reported to the police. Only 8 per cent of rapes and 18 per cent of sexual assaults had been reported. The researchers concluded: 'If 8 per cent of women report rape – one in twelve – it means that criminal statistics based on police reports must be multiplied by twelve to get anywhere near a true picture of what is happening to London women and girls' (Hall 1985, p. 106). The survey is especially revealing with regard to the reasons why such incidents are not reported to the police. In the case of rape, a full 79 per cent of those who did not report the incidents failed to do so because they thought the police would be 'unhelpful or unsympathetic' (p. 110).

Such surveys have shown up the underestimation of violence against women in the area of rape and sexual assault, both by official statistics and by orthodox criminal victimization studies. In this context it is quite remarkable, after two decades of feminist politics and research and the series of frightening reports issuing from rape crisis centres and battered women's refuges, that two progressive writers like Ryan and Sim can accept so uncritically the official figures on violence. There is a general principle at work here: the more vulnerable a group of people are to crime, the less likely are the official figures (whether police statistics or victim reports) to reflect the real situation that they face. The greater the degree of vulnerability, the greater the underestimation. The same analysis could no doubt be applied to another vulnerable and powerless group in society: children. The murder rates for children show that the first year of life is the most dangerous. And because of the ease of concealment – for example, cot deaths possibly fabricated by parents – such figures are certainly a gross underestimate.

If underestimation is a product of power, then just as weaker social groups will find offences committed against them underestimated, then more powerful social groups will find ways of underestimating the number of offences they commit. The question of complaints against the police provides a good illustration. In 1983, 2,216 people made allegations of criminal offences against members of the Metropolitan Police in London. These complaints were, of course, investigated by the police themselves. Of the complaints, 98.6 per cent were unsubstantiated, and the majority of those that were fell into the category of traffic offences. The official record of the police was exemplary to the point of satire: only 0.5 per cent of assault charges were substantiated; no perjury charges were brought; there were no cases of racial discrimination, only one case of mistaken arrest and one of conspiracy. Needless to say, such minuscule levels are ridiculous, given a Metropolitan Police force of over 26,000 officers. It would need a force of angels to achieve such results. But we can be more precise than this. The PSI survey on the Metropolitan Police, commissioned by the police themselves and published in 1983, points in a rather different direction.

A sample of Londoners were asked whether they thought the police fabricated evidence, used violence on suspects held at police stations, used excessive force on arrest and made false records of interviews. We see from Table 8 that an extremely high proportion of Londoners think that the police engage in illegalities. The percentage of respondents making such an assessment increases markedly when ethnic origin, age, and the two combined are taken into consideration. Such assessments also increase if other factors such as unemployment are included, indicating that beliefs in police illegality increase with the degree of powerlessness of a group within

Table 8   Londoners' opinions on police behaviour

% who thought that the police often or occasionally:	All whites	All West Indians	Whites aged 15–24	West Indians aged 15–24
fabricate evidence	37	73	42	75
use violence on suspects	30	71	41	82
use excessive force on arrest	37	73	42	72
make false records of interviews	26	60	30	66

Source: PSI 1983, vol. 1

society. Furthermore, one tenth of all Londoners and almost half of all young West Indians think that such activities occur 'often'. 'These findings,' the PSI report author David Smith writes, 'suggest that there is a complete lack of confidence in the police among at least 1 in 10 of Londoners . . . The lack of confidence in the police among young West Indians can only be described as disastrous' (PSI 1983, vol. 1, pp. 325–6).

Of course, it could be argued that these are merely people's mistaken opinions of the police. Even if this were so, it would tell us something very significant about police relations with the public, but the PSI research team are able to take us further on the issue. They found that 14 per cent of Londoners who believe that the police use excessive force on arrest base their opinion on the fact that it happened to someone they know, or that they actually saw it happen. This represents, as Smith points out, perhaps 700,000 Londoners, 'whom it will be hard to convince that this type of misconduct does not occur'. Once again, according to pattern, 35 per cent of West Indians who claimed that this phenomenon occurs based their belief on similar experience. And if we look at people who have actually been arrested during the five years before the survey, we find very high percentages believing in police misconduct. Thus 57 per cent of people who had been arrested during the previous five years believed that the police use threats in questioning suspects, 32 per cent believed that they use excessive force on arrest, 40 per cent that they use unjustifiable violence at the police station, and 36 per cent that they fabricate evidence.

It is clear, therefore, that a large number of Londoners believe – on the basis of direct observation or knowledge from friends and relatives – that the police act illegally, often using violence. If only a minute proportion of these beliefs represented the truth, the number of criminal complaints substantiated against police officers would be very much higher. Yet, as we have seen, very few complaints are in fact substantiated. In the third volume of their report the PSI researchers noted that only 4.5 per cent of police officers had been the object of a complaint against them, which had been substantiated, over the previous ten years. The powerful in society – among whom the police are to be included – can conceal crimes committed by them and create a situation in which the accusations and beliefs of the less powerful concerning criminal actions against them are hidden and discounted.

Serious crime is underestimated, but not randomly. Crime affecting some groups is underestimated more than others: these are the poor and the powerless sections of society. Crimes of violence against women are one important illustration of this. Likewise, crime committed *by* some groups is underestimated more than crime committed by others. Groups with the power to discount or to hide the crimes they commit can be sure of an underestimation of their activity in the crime statistics.

The Focus of Crime

Crime is sharply focused by geographical area and by social category. In the introduction to this book we showed, with reference to Merseyside, how poor areas of the city are more likely to be victimized than rich areas. We can illustrate this in more detail here with data from the Merseyside survey. The bar chart in Figure 6 shows the percentage of respondents in different areas of the conurbation who were victimized two or more times during the period covered by the survey. As we can see, the highest victimization rate is for inner-city Granby, which has double the rate of the middle-class and 'respectable' suburbs of Ainsdale and Haydock. In between are the poor working-class areas of inner-city Birkenhead, and the outer-city council estates of Northwood in an area of Kirby deserted by industry. Of course, if we broke these areas down into smaller units and compared fashionable middle-class areas with problem estates, we would register even greater disparities of geographical focusing.

Add to this geographical dimension the social one. Certain types of people are more likely to experience crime than others. The PSI report showed that in London an unemployed person is over two and a half times more likely to be a victim of physical attack than an employed person (PSI 1983, vol. 1, p. 62). An Asian, according to the same report, is twice as likely to be a victim of robbery and violent theft as a white. Likewise for age, 'the rate of victimization is more than three times as high among those aged 20–24 as among those aged 60 and over' (p. 59). Crimes of violence are concentrated among younger age groups: 'The victims of physical attacks and assaults are almost exclusively aged under 45. Further, it is mostly young men who are involved in such incidents.'

Women have lower victimization rates than men, but this serves only to illustrate how underestimation and focusing combine. Those offences which impact significantly on women, which are forms of violence against women by men, are

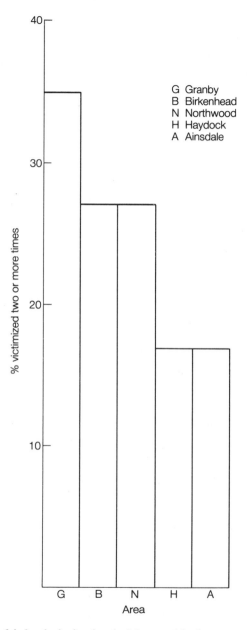

Figure 6   Multiple victimization in Merseyside, by area.
Source: Kinsey 1984

among the most underestimated, as we have seen. Significantly, perhaps, for a common street crime which is less likely to be unrecorded either by criminal victimization surveys or by the official crime statistics – namely, theft from a pocket, briefcase or bag – the PSI survey reported higher victimization for women (p. 59).

Focusing, of course, has a multiplier effect. A young unemployed person belonging to an ethnic minority group and living in an inner-city area is far more likely to experience victimization than a professionally employed middle-aged white man living in a fashionable suburb.

Compounding: The Multiple Problems of the Poor

We have seen, then, that the suggestion that crimes of violence are a small part of all crime ignores both the underestimation and the specific focusing of such crimes. Further support for the argument that violence is indeed a serious problem can be grouped under the heading of 'compounding'. First, those who are the victims of violent crime are also more likely to be victims of property offences, and those who are victims of crime are also more likely to suffer from other social problems. The poor suffer from poverty above all – but also from bad housing, unemployment, pollution, nuisance, *and* crime. So crime is experienced more by people who are already suffering from other social problems, and crimes of violence tend to be experienced by people who are already suffering the impact of other forms of crime.

Some argue that 'corporate crime' – crimes of negligence or fraudulence committed by large companies and institutions – is much more of a problem for working-class people than crime committed by other working-class people. Surely, it might be felt, the problems of pollution, violation of safety regulations by employers, overcrowding and road accidents are more of a problem than street crime and interpersonal violence. But the point is that the poor suffer from more crime than any other section of society, *whatever* the origins of the crime. Crime comes at the poor from all directions. The person most likely to suffer from interpersonal violence in a bar is also the most likely to suffer from an injury at work due to an employer's violation of the factory safety regulations, as well as being the person most likely to suffer as a result of traffic accidents. And, as we have said, even though most acts of interpersonal crime are minor, they have a cumulative effect. The brutalization of a marriage through repeated violence, the thousand small acts of vandalism, though each in itself irritatingly trivial, create intolerable conditions for the tenants of an afflicted council estate already bearing the brunt of other social problems.

Often the understandable focusing on major crimes ignores the fact that they represent the tip of the iceberg of anti-social behaviour. We can see this also in the phenomenon of racial and sexual harassment. As we said in *What Is To Be Done About Law and Order?*:

A lot of the more frequent, everyday, offences are scarcely criminal; they are 'just kids fooling around'. But they are part and parcel of the same appalling aggression towards defenceless people.

A parallel phenomenon to such racist aggression is the sexual harassment of women. Women have to take a considerable amount of sexual harassment at work and in the streets, which severely restricts their ability to move in public spaces, particularly at night. Rape is the end point of the continuum of aggressive sexual behaviour. Its comparative rarity does not indicate the absence of anti-social behaviour towards women. On the contrary, it is a real threat which also symbolises a massive undertow of harassment. (Lea and Young 1984, pp. 57–8)

Differential Vulnerability

Crime has to be looked at not just in terms of the number of offences committed, or of the value of property stolen, but, crucially, in terms of its impact on people's lives. People differ in their ability to resist the impact of crime. To talk in terms of a 'general risk' of being a victim – for example, to say the the 'average person' stands a chance of being burgled once in 30 years – assumes we are all equal in our capacity to resist. Similarly, certain sections of the population are much more vulnerable with regard to crime than others. Merely to say that in the majority of burglaries little of value is stolen is to have precious little understanding of the effect of burglary on those who are poor and socially isolated. To steal a small sum from a poor person may have a dramatic effect on their already precarious financial predicament. This is why the frequently heard argument that a third of recorded burglaries involve less than £25 stolen and two-thirds less than £100, with the conclusion that the problem is therefore grossly exaggerated, is incorrect. The effect is not proportional to the sum lost. It is crucial to understand that it is not possible to gauge from the monetary value of an offence such as burglary whether the crime is relatively trivial or not. The same principle applies to other offences.

It is very easy for middle-class people to suggest that most crimes of property are trivial, since most middle-class people are least vulnerable to such offences in terms of the impact on their lives. Collecting the insurance and buying the new stereo can be a positive pleasure. This probably explains why middle-class commentators distinguish violence as the only really serious crime, claiming at the same time that it occurs comparatively rarely. In reality both violence and property crimes have a substantial impact on the weaker sections of society, and less effect on the lives of the well-heeled and insured.

We conclude this chapter where we began: with the seriousness of crime as a problem – and, we emphasize, a serious problem for those sections of society that the Labour Party should be mobilizing and defending. If certain sections of the middle-class radical intelligentsia wish to challenge this fact

then they end up, as we have suggested, echoing the senti-
ments of the – also middle- and upper-class, and male –
professional elites which operate the state apparatus. Law and
order, we are suggesting, is a radical issue. It is an issue for the
poor and the old, least able to resist the impact of crimes that
to statisticians far away from the inner cities and decaying
council estates may appear trivial. It is an issue for ethnic
minorities suffering racial harassment and racial attacks. It is
an issue for women suffering levels of male harassment and
violence both inside and outside the home that are grossly
underestimated by the official statistics. All these social
groups, despite their many differing interests, have a common
interest in combating crime.

4

Letting the Police off the Hook

The findings of the Home Office Research Unit on crime and police effectiveness . . . come as no surprise to those who have studied this area in the last few years. Indeed, the central conclusion that policing can only play a limited role in preventing crime, has become accepted wisdom in some quarters. Within the Home Office itself, this message has for some time now been pushed gently under the noses of successive ministers. *The British Crime Survey* said it: other research documents have said it. Yet politically, the message is still a difficult one to get across.

. . . Research indicates that any type of policing can make only a limited impact upon crime whose causes are complex; as the report puts it, influences or experiences in the family, at school, at work, or among neighbours and associates are thought by most informed commentators to determine crime levels to a far greater extent than any strategies adopted by the police. To a certain extent, the police are taking this message on board. They are now admitting that there are limits to their effectiveness. (*Guardian* editorial, 25 April 1984)

So there we have it: the police are off the hook and the crisis in policing is abated by the simple discovery that crime levels and policing strategies are unrelated. Inherent in the *Guardian* commentary on the Home Office study *(Crime and Police Effectiveness)* is the common liberal notion that if crime is the result of social determinants then there is little that society can do about it as long as those determinants persist. Add to this the obvious point that deterrence is largely ineffective, given that the police cannot be everywhere, and we have a recipe for inaction – or for placing the responsibility for crime control on other institutions.

There are two problems with this view. First, offenders are not ineluctably propelled by social conditions. They have individual moral choice within the context of the circumstances which beset them. After all, even though crime is distinctly related to poverty, only a tiny proportion of the poor at any given time commit crimes. Crime is a subjective choice in a given objective situation. And deterrence is not about the fear of being caught red-handed; it is concerned with the certainty of being detected in the long run. The police can play a vital part in this process, but – and this is the crucial point – only when they have the support of the public with respect to reporting and witnessing incidents. Police action against offenders should involve the minimum coercion necessary to apprehend them: this would mean the provision of firm but fair limits to police powers. At present, however, police action often involves much more than that: undue force and unfair procedures which exacerbate the sense of injustice among the community and end up making the police more ineffective.

The *Guardian*, moreover, misinterpreted the Home Office study: its actual conclusion was that *extra* policing will not be cost-effective in controlling crime and that beat policing in general is grossly ineffective. Let us take the first contention. Ken Pease of the University of Manchester comments, in a letter to the *Guardian*:

The sort of relationship described between the extent of something (in this case, policing) and its result (in this case, lawfulness) is familiar, for example, in the use of vitamin supplementation in health care, and of yeast in baking. Up to a (low) critical level the ingredient is helpful. Above that level it does not become helpful. (30 April 1984)

Of course, no one, outside perhaps of the Police Federation, would argue that what is necessary is indeed more police, but Pease's vitamin analogy is severely flawed. For the problem is that the present supplement has, in any case, precious little positive effect on society. The expensive vitamins we have prescribed for ourselves do not increase vitality – in fact they seem to be making matters worse. This is not an argument for discarding vitamins: it is an argument for better quality control. The argument against beat policing (police officers on foot patrol) is now widely held. Despite the fact that the public like beat policing – all surveys on the subject show a wide demand for 'putting the bobby back on the beat' – academic research seems to indicate that the only cogent argument for foot patrols is to give the public a sense of security. But such a generalization is not a universal law, as the Home Office researchers seem to suggest. The caveat which they were unable, or perhaps too tactful, to add is 'in the present political context'. In that context, in which the police officer is unaccountable to the public and where his or her actions are self-initiated rather than a direct response to public demand, we have another recipe for disaster. Operations in which substantial numbers of people are stopped and searched in the street very often stem from nothing more than boredom on the part of police officers. Their targets are frequently dictated by racial prejudice, and the result is the alienation from the police of the most relevant sections of the community – relevant, that is, as far as crime control is concerned. As we have said, the sections of the public most likely to be harassed and caught in stop and search operations are precisely those that have most information about crime and whose cooperation is essential in solving it. The beat policing system is certainly not likely to lead to an increase in clear-up rates. On the contrary, by alienating the community from the police, it contributes to a decline. But in a political context in which the police had the confidence of the local community, beat policing would lead to increased contact with that community, greater information flow to the police from the public, and an increased clear-up rate. The same institution – beat

policing – can have very different effects in different social and
political circumstances. There is no single, absolute effect of
such a policy. To suppose that there is is a crucial flaw in the
reasoning of the Home Office research. Abstract generalizations about a particular policy such as police patrolling
styles, with 'evidence' drawn willy-nilly from Idaho to Shef-
field, are a useless exercise – after all, they have beat policing
in Soweto too.

The Wilson–Kelling Hypothesis

A much more sophisticated position on the relationship
between beat policing and crime control has been evolved in
the United States over the last few years. It is the work of
James Q. Wilson – the author of a best-selling book in North
America, *Thinking About Crime* (1975), and in 1985 the chair-
man of the working party on the control of crime set up by the
Reagan administration – and his associate George Kelling, a
former director of the Police Foundation and a major re-
searcher in the area of beat policing. Their work has had
considerable influence both in the United States and in Home
Office circles in Britain (see Clarke and Hough 1984; Wilson
and Kelling 1982). Baldly stated, the hypothesis maintains
that beat policing is effective not through a direct effect on the
control of crime, but rather in facilitating the maintenance of
social order. Furthermore, where disorderly behaviour (for
example, that of drunks, rowdy youths) is not controlled, the
neighbourhood enters a spiral of decline in which the law-
abiding emigrate from the area, informal social controls
weaken, and crime itself begins to rise. So police involvement
in 'order maintenance' facilitates, in the long run, the process
of crime control. Police presence facilitates the growth of
informal neighbourhood controls on crime by giving the area
a general sense of security.

Such a hypothesis must be seen in the general context of

Wilson's work, which has profoundly shaped both academic criminology and policy-making in the United States in the recent period. Wilson divides police work into three types: law enforcement, order maintenance and public service. The latter is concerned with traffic control, rescuing cats from trees, distributing lost property, and so on. Wilson sees it as mere historical contingency that the police should be concerned with such work and quickly eliminates it from his analysis. It is the distinction between law enforcement and order maintenance that is central to his argument. For Wilson,

the problem of order, more than the problem of law enforcement, is central. . . . The patrolman's role is defined more by his responsibility for *maintaining order* than by his responsibility for enforcing the law. By 'order' is meant the absence of disorder, and by disorder is meant behavior that either disturbs or threatens to disturb the public peace or that involves face to face conflict among two or more persons . . . a noisy drunk, a rowdy teenager shouting or racing his car in the middle of the night, a loud radio in the apartment next door, a panhandler [down-and-out] soliciting money from passers by, persons wearing eccentric clothes and unusual hair styles loitering in public places – all these are examples of behavior which the public (an onlooker, a neighbor, the community at large) may disapprove of and ask the patrolman to 'put a stop to'. Needless to say the drunk, the teenager, the persons next door, the panhandler and the hippies are likely to take a different view of the matter, to suggest that people 'mind their own business', and to be irritated with the cop who intervenes. On the other hand a fight, a tavern brawl and an assault on an unfaithful lover are kinds of behavior that even the participants are not likely to condone. Thus they may agree that the police have a right to intervene, but they are likely to disagree over who is to blame and thus against whom the police ought to act.

Some or all of these examples of disorderly behavior involve infractions of the law; any intervention by the police is at least under cover of the law and in fact might be viewed as an enforcement of the law. A judge, examining the matter after the fact, is likely to see the issue wholly in these terms. But the patrolman does not. Though he may use the law to make an arrest, just as often he will do something else, such as tell people to 'knock it off', 'break it up' or 'go home and sober up'. (Wilson 1968, pp. 16–17)

Order is a priority in police time; it involves, Wilson calculates, three times as much time as law enforcement. It is a more difficult task and yet it is the job at which the police are most effective. Extra police on the beat may not reduce the crime rate immediately, as George Kelling in his study of Newark, New Jersey, showed, but it considerably reduces people's fear of crime. There are, according to this line of argument, several reasons for this apparent paradox. First, fear of crime is closely related to fear of disorder, and disorder itself frightens people. Second, in the long run disorder begets more disorder, and more disorder produces crime. That is, when order maintenance breaks down, the natural informal control mechanisms – the social antibodies of the community – are weakened, and real increases in crime ensue. Thus the public are not at all irrational in welcoming beat policing. It helps maintain order in their area, which is not only a major gain in itself, but in the long run it helps the community to maintain its informal mechanisms of control, which limit crime itself. Indeed some American research (for instance, that of Wesley Skogan in his study of 36 housing projects in inner-city areas) claims to have confirmed the argument (Skogan 1983).

Historically, the police function, from city nightwatchman onwards, has given priority to order. It is only, according to Wilson and Kelling, in response to the rapid rise in crime in the United States in the recent period that crime control has become of major importance. This has involved a shift from the police officer as maintainer of order, improvising the ground rules in accordance with the customs and habits of the community, to the police officer as functionary of the rule of law, directed by the justice department and hemmed in by legal rules and official procedures. This transition has been to the detriment of order. Strict justice and the rules of due process do not facilitate the maintenance of order. Wilson and Kelling write:

Until quite recently in many states, and even today in some places, the police make arrests on such charges as 'suspicious persons' or 'vagrancy' or 'public drunkenness' – charges with scarcely any legal meaning. These charges exist not because society wants judges to punish vagrants or drunks but because it wants an officer to . . . remove undesirable persons from a neighborhood when informal efforts to preserve order in the streets have failed . . .

Once we begin to think of all aspects of police work as involving the application of universal rules under special procedures, we inevitably ask: 'What constitutes an undesirable person?' . . . A strong and commendable desire to see that people are treated fairly makes us worry about allowing the police to rout persons who are undesirable by some vague or parochial standard. A growing and not so commendable utilitarianism leads us to doubt that any behavior that does not 'hurt' another person should be made illegal. And thus many of us who watch over the police are reluctant to allow them to perform, in the only way they can, a function that every neighborhood wants them to perform. (Wilson and Kelling 1982, p. 35)

What is necessary, then, is to award priority to order, and not to judge the police solely on their ability as crime fighters. We must concentrate our resources in those areas 'at the tipping point' and 'where the public order is deteriorating but not unreclaimable' – not necessarily those with the highest crime rates, which may have gone past the point of no return. Police officers must be trained in managing street life as much as in law and due process. And we must, Wilson and Kelling insist, oppose campaigns to decriminalize the so-called harmless behaviours: 'Public drunkenness, street prostitution, and pornographic displays can destroy a community more quickly than any team of professional burglars' (p. 38).

It is important to note the political targets of such an analysis. Wilson and Kelling are opposed to traditional conservative policies of heavy policing. But, more revealing, they also set themselves against liberal and socialist notions of crime control. First, they oppose the decriminalization of minor crimes and so-called crimes without victims. Second, their analysis widens the sphere for social control by seeing the control of deviant behaviour both illegal *and* legal as important in the maintenance of order. Third, it sees the liberal emphasis on rights and due process as counterproductive and is critical of both the possibility and the desirability of tight management controls on the police. Lastly, the analysis emphasizes social control by both the community and the police as the key to crime control, rather than hoping to reduce crime through measures aimed at the elimination of poverty and deprivation.

Wilson and Kelling's work certainly has a kernel of truth, but their analysis contains both a degree of obfuscation and a one-sidedness which make it particularly pernicious. Let us look at the implications of their analysis in relation to British policing.

It is possible to concede that crime is a problem, to stress that it hurts the working class more than the middle class, but yet to deny that police effectiveness should be couched in terms of crime control. As Pauline Morris and Kevin Heal (1981) in their comprehensive review of the relationship between policing and crime control caution us, it is important to recognize that police effectiveness and crime control effectiveness should not be confused. And Dr P. A. J. Waddington from Reading University, in a letter to the *Guardian*, while agreeing that 'crime disproportionately further disadvantages the already deprived', goes on to argue that:

it is wrong to suggest that police effectiveness should be measured in terms of crime-fighting success: the clear-up rate.

While it is true that those living in the most socially deprived districts of our large cities suffer disproportionately from serious crimes, like burglary and 'mugging', what really diminishes the quality of life in these areas is the endemic rowdyism, hooliganism, vandalism, drunkenness and a host of supposedly 'victimless' offences . . .

It is is responding to complaints from those living in these areas about these continual depredations, that the police spend much of their time. Nor does it stop there, for the manifestation of social deprivation, disorganisation and decay extend well beyond narrowly defined crime. It is because the police do more, much more and of greater social value, than detecting offenders that any assessment of their effectiveness based solely upon crime fighting is a misguided distortion.

What the police actually do, as I have been observing over the past few months, is to quell violent 'domestic' disputes; quieten noisy and rowdy youths; pacify drunken disorderliness; and those myriad other 'peace-keeping' tasks which they are called upon, by the public, to perform. (*Guardian*, 9 May 1984)

In criticizing this type of argument we may start with Wilson's division of a police officer's duty into law enforcement, order maintenance and public service. We can eliminate the public service role and wholeheartedly agree with the contention that such a role does not inherently belong to police work. Wilson himself sees 'no reason in principle why these services could not be priced and sold on the market. It is only a matter of historical accident and community convenience that they are provided by the police; one can just as easily imagine them sold by a private profit-making firm ("Emergency Services Inc.").' We would, of course, allocate such responsibilities to the most obvious and logical agency: the social services, together with a commensurate transfer of funds from police budgets.

Let us take a closer look at the distinction Wilson makes in *Varieties of Police Behavior* between law enforcement and order maintenance. Table 9, taken from Wilson (1968), shows the types of citizen calls on the police department in Syracuse, New York, over a week in June 1966.

What becomes immediately apparent is that a large proportion of what Wilson classifies as order maintenance calls are *in fact* concerned with law enforcement. This includes areas where the police do intercede, as for example with gang violence, assaults and fights, and areas where they do not, as with family trouble (that is, domestic disputes). The distinction between order maintenance and law enforcement is based, as Wilson acknowledges, on the pragmatic distinctions and practical difficulties faced and made by police officers, rather than on any matter of law. It is difficult to see, for example, why, in real terms, an assault is a question of order

Table 9   *Citizen complaints radioed to patrol vehicles, Syracuse Police Department, 3–9 June 1966*[a]

Calls		Number in sample	Full count (sample multiplied by 5)	%
Information gathering		69	345	22.1
Book and check	2			
Get a report	67			
Service		117	585	37.5
Accidents, illnesses, ambulance calls	42			
Animals	8			
Assist a person	1			
Drunk person	8			
Escort vehicle	3			
Fire, power line or tree down	26			
Lost or found person or property	23			
Property damage	6			
Order maintenance		94	479	30.1
Gang disturbance	50			
Family trouble	23			
Assault, fight	9			
Investigation	8			
Neighbour trouble	4			
Law enforcement		32	160	10.3
Burglary in progress	9			
Check a car	5			
Open door, window	8			
Prowler	6			
Make an arrest	4			
TOTALS		312	1,560	100.0

[a]Based on a one-fifth sample of a week's calls.
Source: Wilson 1968, p. 18

maintenance while checking a car is law enforcement. If Wilson is suggesting that minor crime is important one can only agree with him, but then we are dealing with illegality, and legal procedures must govern police behaviour in such situations.

The question of domestic violence illustrates even more clearly the arbitrary nature of Wilson's distinction between order maintenance and law enforcement. 'Family trouble' constituted a large percentage of the so-called order maintenance cases in Wilson's 1966 sample. As we have noted, the distinction between order maintenance and law enforcement is based on nothing more than police culture and operational practice, which are heavily influenced by cultural norms. Wilson notes (1968, p. 24) that the police dislike dealing with domestic disputes, and in Britain Reiner (1978) notes how police officers include domestic disputes alongside things like traffic control as frustrating departures from 'real police work'. In 1978 Tony Faragher observed Staffordshire police officers on domestic violence incidents. Of the 26 cases he observed,

> ten [38 per cent] contained an infringement of the legal code which, had the police so wished, could have formed the basis for a charge and subsequent arrest. In more detail five of these ten cases involved assault . . . all would, under the terms laid down in the Offences Against the Person Act 1861, be properly classified as section 47 offences – assault occasioning actual bodily harm. In two out of these cases an arrest was made, although in one of the two it was clear that the arrest was made primarily because of the presence of an observer. (Faragher 1985, p. 113)

Faragher points out that the Staffordshire police had issued written instructions to their officers to the effect that arrest in such cases must be automatic, but that 'the scope for individual discretion [by police officers], namely the power to redefine events so as to disguise the fact of assault, means that in practice such orders can effectively be countermanded' (p. 123). So in these cases of domestic disputes involving male violence against women, despite formal instructions regarding such cases as clearly falling into the category of law enforcement, the sexist culture of police officers themselves redefined the incidents as coming within a non-law-enforcement category – and did this moreover, in a way which poses a problem for Wilson and Kelling's argument, for the police didn't really want to be involved, did not see such matters as real police work. We shall return to this issue in later chapters.

Thus 'order maintenance' is something of an ideological category – it turns out to consist of those crimes which the police don't want to be involved in. The police contribution to maintaining order in a local community should be precisely to provide an effective crime-fighting service. One is dumbfounded by Peter Waddington's suggestion that the British police should be judged by their successes at policing the 'order' problems which blight the lives of the poor, when it is precisely the *crimes* involved in such problems of social disorder which are most under-represented in crime statistics and with which the police are most loath to deal. The most vulnerable categories of our society – the lower working class, the unemployed, women, ethnic minorities – get short shrift in terms of police service, both for 'real crimes' (as defined by police practices and preferences) and what Wilson and Kelling and their British adherents insist on seeing as problems of 'order'.

Those incidents which might be regarded as disturbances but which do not involve illegalities, are simply not areas in which the police should intervene. The vast majority of police-initiated stops of individuals in public is either for actions which are perfectly legal or for illegalities of an extremely trivial nature. And here, as we have pointed out, the poor do get a large amount of attention from the police, of a type which creates alienation, thereby making effective policing more difficult. Yet Wilson and Kelling seem positively to welcome such police illegality. Their recipe for order would, in fact, increase disorder and disaffection from the law.

Just as Wilson and Kelling give priority to police definitions of 'real' crime and 'order maintenance', they analyse the relationship between the police and the law in terms of the definition of the situation as seen by the police themselves. So in analysing the difficulties that the police officer encounters in enforcing the law, they begin explicitly with the police view of the street and how this circumscribes the degree to which police behaviour can be modified by organizational directives from within the police. The concerns of both the judiciary and the public, of procedural rules and legal rights, are relegated to second place or seen as counterproductive. The day-to-day problems of policing have, of course, to be taken into account if we are to understand both what occurs and what is possible in police work. But to focus on the police aspect at the expense of public priorities, the rule of law and democratic accountability is conceptually mistaken and politically dangerous. At the very least, it grossly underestimates the possible impact of legal rules on police behaviour (see Baldwin and Kinsey 1985) and the possibilities of change. Thus the exercise of police discretion, which is logically necessary and ethically desirable under clearly stipulated rules and limits, as we shall argue further on in this book, becomes, in the Wilson–Kelling analysis, an uncontested virtue whose social benefits are seen to be stymied by due process and legal limitation.

Wilson and Kelling represent the most sophisticated justification for letting the police off the hook by replacing the usual performance indicator – the clear-up rate for crime – with that of order maintenance. We have no quarrel with order maintenance, as long as by this is meant the control of illegalities – and at this point the concept of order maintenance, as far as policing is concerned, recedes into that of the control of crime. By creating a false distinction, Wilson and Kelling take the pressure off criticism of the police for low crime clear-up, while at the same time justifying the extension of police control into any area of behaviour regarded as 'deviant' by the passing police officer. This sort of behaviour is precisely what lies at the heart of the current crisis in policing and the falling clear-up rate. As we have noted, it is public alienation from the police that has led to a fall in the flow of information about crime and a decline in clear-ups. That alienation is due to police behaviour which under the Wilson–Kelling analysis might well be seen as 'order maintenance'. So we are back where we began, with the crisis in the clear-up rate.

5

Neighbourhood Crime Watch

The initiatives that the police have taken in recent years can conveniently be divided into 'hard' measures aiming at strengthening police powers and technology, and 'soft' measures aiming at incorporating the public at large and other social service agencies both as sources of information for the police and to take over some responsibility for crime control. In this chapter we look at one 'soft measure', neighbourhood crime watch.

Neighbourhood Watch is an American import, so it is useful to begin by looking at one of the most exemplary such schemes in the United States – the one developed in Detroit. This city, known as the homicide capital of the United States, became the location for an extraordinary experiment in crime control.

Coleman Young, a radical democrat, and black, was elected mayor on a pledge to deal with the problems of crime and policing in the city. In 1976 he appointed a new chief of police, William Hart, and their agreed aims were more effective crime prevention and apprehension of offenders and, most crucially, to build a police department which reflected and was trusted by the community. Their joint task was to achieve these goals against a background of severe social and economic urban deprivation and declining local government resources. Hart and Young expanded the Crime Prevention Section of the police department from a staff of two in 1975 to a division with 150 officers and an operating budget of 4.5 million dollars in 1982. It is currently the largest such unit in the United States, and has the best reputation in the crime prevention field. It was under this rubric that the Neighbourhood Watch schemes, emerged.

While radically expanding existing crime prevention schemes, Commissioner Hart was also resolved to act firmly in the more traditional field of the apprehension of criminals. This involved increasing the efficiency of the courts by ensuring that three quarters of the outstanding felony warrants were enacted, and increasing the efficiency of the police by concentrating on repeat offenders and career criminals. Lastly, and very significantly, they set themselves the task of creating a police force which reflected and was responsive to the demands of the community. This involved moving towards a more ethnically balanced police force – including bringing in Arab–Americans and Mexican–Americans – setting up an independent police complaints body with real powers, and establishing in each neighbourhood High Street mini-police stations to offer their services to the public. As Hart put it: 'We're not an army of occupation. We're citizens of the community. And since all the problems of the community eventually become police problems, that makes us social workers and social scientists too. Positive change in Detroit only came about when the police attitude and image changed.' (Pollock 1983, p. 25).

Such a three-pronged tactic, then, while maintaining a stress on apprehension, moved its emphasis towards prevention and, most importantly, occurred in an administration which was radical and had the power democratically to control policing. That is, it controlled not only the appointment of the chief of police but police appointments in general, and it set up a complaints board independently of the police.

It is in this context that the Neighbourhood Watch scheme (NWS) was launched. Of course, many North American – and the more recent British – projects carry the title NWS, but the Detroit experiment was something different. As Inspector

Humphrey, chief of the expanded Crime Prevention Section, put it: 'Neighborhood Watch means different things to different people around the country and I am personally skeptical of a lot of the programs going under the title' (Pollock 1983). The Detroit NWS consists of four components:

1   self-protection: strategies for avoiding victimization in public places

2   burglary protection: methods of best safeguarding one's house

3   property identification: methods of marking one's property so that it is less attractive to a thief and more easily recovered if stolen

4   crime reporting: instructions on how to report crime or suspicious events to the police which will maximize police efficiency (usually a checklist of items to look for).

Thus the emphasis is largely on public education and, in the case of the first three items, on the prevention of crime rather than on the apprehension of the criminal. A lot of this education is obvious yet vital. For example, it is calculated in the United States that 35–40 per cent of burglaries occur through unlocked doors and windows; so we see that the most elementary precautions can be extremely efficacious in preventing burglary.

The extent to which the Detroit NWS has spread, and the level of education, are extremely impressive. John Pollock summed it up in the Figgie Report:

Detroit has conducted more than 10,000 crime prevention programs, reaching upwards of 600,000 people directly. Over 3,500 Neighborhood Watch groups have been organized; 67 Business Watches and 35 Apartment Watches have been instituted. Crime prevention officers have carried out in excess of 6,000 individual security surveys. About 650 special crime prevention programs have been held for schoolchildren, reaching approximately 175,000 students. Some 400 special programs have been implemented for senior citizens, touching about 29,000 people. (1983, p. 32)

A vital element of the Detroit NWS is its basis in the infrastructure of the community.

Neighborhood Watch undoubtedly has roots in the social movements of the 1960s and 1970s. Groups formed to advance special interests like minority and women's rights proved that unified actions could produce positive change. Likewise, the era witnessed the founding of community groups to improve local schools, neighborhoods, etc. Neighborhood Watch is a derivation of the community action group, which focuses on the residents' mutual concern for avoiding criminal victimization. (p. 31)

Let us note what is exceptional about the Detroit NWS. It sprang up within a radical administration pledged to change the nature of policing in the city, and with the democratic powers available to do so. The scale of the operation was considerable. It was based on a real community rather than a quasi-community of 'respectable' citizens, linked together almost totally through their contacts with the police. And, finally, it was very carefully monitored in the Crary-St Mary's experiment.

The Crary-St Mary's Experiment

In the spring of 1977 the Crime Prevention Section of the Detroit police set out 'to prove or disprove the idea that a comprehensive crime prevention program involving both the police and citizens would reduce crime' (Pollock 1983, p. 32) They took two neighbourhoods in Detroit about four miles apart, with similar demographic and crime characteristics. In one, Crary-St Mary's, they instigated an extensive crime prevention programme; in the other, they maintained identical police services but no programme.

Crary-St Mary's was a residential area with a population of about 13,000 – 65 per cent white and 35 per cent non-white – a median income of $15,000 a year, and 20 per cent were senior citizens. During the 1970s its population had changed dramatically, with a growing elderly population, mostly white, and a shift amongst the youth from predominantly white to predominantly black. Unemployment was estimated as high as 50 per cent, and crime was rising, particularly where burglary and street robbery were concerned.

First let us consider the crime prevention programme, which was a considerable success (Table 10).

Table 10   Crime prevention measures adopted by Crary-St Mary's inhabitants (%)

	Pre-test (%)	Post-test (%)
Measures taken to protect house	28	60
Marking possessions	28	62
Arrangements to watch neighbours' houses while away	72	89

Source: Pollock 1983

Then look at the results of the crime prevention programme over the period 1977–79 when compared to the pre-test period and to the control area (Table 11).

Thus the crime rate in Crary-St Mary's had gone down 58 per cent while in the control neighbourhood only 11 per cent. The decline in the control neighbourhood's crime rate may have been attributable to the general crime prevention programme in Detroit but, whatever, the cause, it is significantly smaller than the decline in Crary-St Mary's. Furthermore, the scale of the decline was over a wide range of crimes.

Table 11   Extent of crime at Crary-St Mary's and in control neighbourhood

1   *At Crary-St Mary's*

	1977 (pre-test)	*1979*	*Change (%)*
Rape	10	4	−60
Robbery	57	25	−56
Breaking and entering	253	97	−61
Larceny	17	9	−53
Larceny from cars	99	49	−51
Purse-snatching	31	12	−61
TOTAL REPORTED CRIME	467	196	−58

Source: Pollock 1983

2   *In control neighbourhood*

	1977 (pre-test)	*1979*	*Change (%)*
Rape	8	8	0
Robbery	52	43	−17
Breaking and entering	206	180	−12
Larceny	6	9	+50
Larceny from cars	94	89	−5
Purse-snatching	7	4	−32
TOTAL REPORTED CRIME	373	333	−11

Source: Pollock 1983

The decline in crime was corroborated in a sample survey which included a question on criminal victimization with regard to burglary. Here the rate of victimization had dropped from the extremely high figure of 24 per cent over a two-year period, to 5 per cent. Not only was the crime rate reduced, but, as we see from Table 12, people's fear of crime was considerably reduced.

Table 12   Fear of crime at Crary-St Mary's before and after the crime prevention programme

Individuals:	Pre-test (%)	Post-test (%)
who were very fearful of crime	40	12
who felt very safe at night	6	30
whose perception of crime had decreased	17	45

We see from Table 13 a considerable change in people's confidence in the police.

Table 13   Confidence in police as expressed by people's perceptions of police behaviour

Individuals who:	Pre-test (%)	Post-test (%)
thought police doing a good job	40	75
thought police doing poor job	6	1
were very satisfied with police after reporting a crime	20	35
were not at all satisfied	10	5

Now if confidence in the police had risen considerably, we would expect a higher rate of crime-reporting. Furthermore, we know from the victimization survey that there exists a considerable dark figure of burglaries unknown to the police: perhaps only one sixth of the total were reported to the police in 1977. If this were so, there would be every possibility that improved police–public relations would result in a *rise* in reported crime. But as we have seen, this was not the case, and this further confirms the fact that a real and dramatic drop in the actual (compared to the known) crime rate occurred in Crary-St Mary's.

The Effect of the Experiment on Community Activity

Lastly, attendance at least once a year at community or 'block' club meetings increased from 27 per cent in the pre-test to 100 per cent in the post-test period. Of course, this result must be treated with caution in that the crime prevention programme itself instituted meetings, but overall the finding that the NWS augments existing community structures is corroborated. As *The Figgie Report* put it 'Wherever Neighbourhood Watch appears, its impact upon the community is always greater than the sum of its parts' (Pollock 1983, p. 32). All in all, the Detroit NWS scheme has had a considerable impact. An area with an extremely high crime rate, racially and generationally mixed, and with a low average income is perhaps the most difficult test of the NWS concept. If it can work in Detroit it can work anywhere, it might be argued. However, several caveats must be made.

Some Caveats about the Detroit Neighbourhood Watch Scheme

First, take the *political* aspect. The NWS was set up in the context of a radical administration with considerable democratic powers over policing. Thus the alienation of the public from the police was assuaged not only by the crime prevention programme and its consequent publicity, but by the palpable movement towards police accountability. It is not at all clear how effective such schemes would be in districts without such democratic provisions; or, to be more specific, NWS may be effective in middle-class areas which have a high degree of confidence in the police, but not so effective in poor areas where there is deep alienation and no direct political control over the police force.

Second, from the *social* point of view, the base 'community' organization at Crary-St Mary's was very strong and pre-existed the NWS. A community council was formed in 1971 to ensure that the demographic changes occurring would lead to racial integration rather than disorganization. As *The Figgie Report* put it:

Most American communities probably do not have a base organization like the Crary-St Mary's Community Council. The CSCC was founded in 1971, when the demographic profile of the community started changing rapidly. A core group of activists organized around the belief that the racial integration of the neighborhood should not mean the ruin of the community.

For over ten years the CSCC has been extraordinarily diligent in a wide range of community projects which achieved effective results – clean-ups and beautification campaigns eliminating nuisances such as abandoned automobiles, monitoring the enforcement of zoning restrictions, overseeing local real estate practices, providing activities for youth and senior citizens, etc. The CSCC membership has remained strong over the years and reflects the black–white ratio of the community. It publishes a monthly newsletter, publicizes community events, and generally is a powerful force for communication and organization in the area.

The Detroit Police Department Crime Prevention Section integrated their activities with this sturdy network provided by the CSCC, with clear, impressive and enviable success. The question arises, however, as to what can be done in a community that has no strong organization such as the CSCC. (Pollock 1983, p. 40)

A cohesive community has the information and the ability to communicate to the police. But what happens if community is lacking? *The Figgie Report* is contradictory about this, for earlier it notes optimistically:

In instances where the natural controls of residents' behaviors have broken down or have never existed, the Neighborhood Watch concept seems to be partially filling the vacuum. It defines a community (a block); it brings people together around a common cause (fear of crime); it draws them into cooperative action (learning about how to avoid victimization, sharing 'Operation identification' engravers); and it ideally creates a sense of unified responsibility (a safe community is one in which you can trust your neighbors to be on the lookout for suspicious activity and to report such events to the proper authorities). (p. 32)

This may be the case – perhaps an NWS is a catalyst which helps rebuild the community. However, we need to know the conditions under which this is possible, particularly as areas with very low community involvement often have the highest crime rates.

Third, consider the question of *police commitment*. Over the experimental period the Detroit police invested an extra-ordinary level of commitment into Crary-St Mary's. It would have been difficult, if not impossible, to apply such resources equally over Detroit. But, as we have seen, the crime rate in the control area also went down – if to a smaller degree – and although, since the end of the experiment (1979), there has been less police department involvement in Crary-St Mary's, there has been no significant turnaround in crime curtailment. However, the question remains: how long can such a level of police activity based on a substructure of community organiz-ation be maintained, and how applicable is the Detroit experiment to other areas? Furthermore, does concentrating police in one area increase the crime rate in others?

The fourth caveat concerns the question of *displacement*, which refers to the process whereby policing a given area merely shifts criminal activity to an adjacent area. Sergeant Barbien of the Crime Prevention Section was adamant that displacement from Crary-St Mary's did not occur: 'I really don't believe there has been displacement going on here. Our experience indicates that there are a few transient burglars. Most of the crimes traced in the experiment are typically committed by neighborhood people' (Pollock 1983, p. 39). And Inspector Humphrey makes the following contrast: 'Professional criminals probably can't be stopped, but in most crime we see – probably 90 per cent – the criminal is an amateur and an opportunist and lives four or five blocks from where the crime is committed. When our crime prevention programs are done right, they don't displace crime. We're changing the environment. And the environment changes attitudes and behavior' (p. 43). Given that most crime is, in fact, very localized, this is probably true. Furthermore, given the comparative poverty of Crary-St Mary's it is unlikely that professional burglars, who *are* transient, would have bothered to work in the area in the first place.

However, as Pauline Morris and Kevin Heal (1981) have observed, it is likely that displacement is a much more complex phenomenon than has been previously thought. Certain crimes may displace to adjacent areas, and it would be valuable to compare the differential crime rates over a range of crimes, in a test and in an adjacent area.

Lastly, we must consider the *relationship between the public and the police*:

The police department looks at the community as well-meaning amateurs. They may think that we have some role to play, like attending community forums and such, but they really don't think we have a serious input when it comes to serious decisions such as where the cops ought to be, where the crime spots are, etc. They just don't want to deal with it that way. (Brenda McLane of the Michigan Avenue Community Organization in Pollock 1983, p.42)

The police ask the community to provide information and to protect themselves and their property. They, as experts, deal with the task at hand, while the public 'cooperates'. Now, given that a high proportion of crimes are of a very minor nature, there are good reasons for arguing that internal intervention may often be preferable to involving the police. That is, the community associations should be able to determine the threshold beyond which police action should intervene. Furthermore, although the police instruct the public as to what crime prevention precautions should be taken, there seems little scope for the public to transmit knowledge of crime control to the police, let alone to immediately affect policy. Yet a well organized community has a considerable information stock which can be of great benefit to policing.

Neighbourhood Watch in Britain

The setting-up of Neighbourhood Watch schemes in Britain involved police officers from this country going on study tours to learn about some of the American schemes. But while the organizational aspect of Neighbourhood Watch can be easily imported, some of the background factors present in the Detroit scheme that we have looked at are largely absent here. Indeed one of them, greater police accountability to the local community, has been strongly resisted by the police leadership in Britain. And the local networks of tenants' and community organizations, which in Detroit were rooted in the Civil Rights struggles of the 1960s, are also far weaker in working-class areas in British cities.

The absence of these two factors is likely to make British Neighbourhood Watch a very different institution from the American one that we have just looked at. In the absence of police accountability to local authorities for general policy matters, it is largely the police who decide when and where to establish such schemes, and their viability. The police may be approached by groups of residents to set up a scheme, but this is much more likely to be in middle-class than in poor, run-down inner-city areas where crime is rampant and the population is alienated from the police. The police may well attempt initially to set up schemes in poor areas. Indeed, a Home Office Crime Prevention Unit guide to police officers stresses: 'There may be a temptation in police-led schemes to look to communities which are fairly well organized, yet these might not be the ones in greatest need of community partici- pation programmes. Inner-city estates and other areas of economic and social deprivation associated with high incidences of crime should not be overlooked' (Home Office 1984b, pp. 3–4). But the point is simply that, in a deprived area, the police have neither the expertise nor the considerable *additional manpower* required to establish, in the manner of social and community workers, forms of crime prevention that require some community cohesion. It can therefore be expected that though the police may attempt to set up schemes in poor inner-city areas, such schemes will have a very high failure rate.

The worst result of a situation like this would be a 'displacement effect' of crime from areas with organized Neighbourhood Watch schemes to those without. In the Detroit scheme, as we have noted, the police were of the opinion that displacement was minimal. But the Crary-St Mary's area of Detroit was a poor area. The transient burglar is probably more a phenomenon of middle-class areas. If successful Neighbourhood Watch schemes (employing property- marking systems) in middle-class areas push burglars out into adjacent working-class areas, crime could well increase in the latter areas. Little research has so far been done on this in Britain, but what scanty evidence there is, is conflicting. And anyway, the same effect might result from police action. With any such scheme that forces criminals back into poorer areas, the other side of the coin is that, having set up schemes in middle-cass areas in their division, the police may service them much more effectively in terms of answering telephone calls and speed of response, regarding burglaries in such areas as more 'solvable' (due to property-marking) and so on. The end result, given no increases in police manpower, would be a decisive diversion of resources away from poorer areas and a further deterioration in service.

In the Crary-St Mary's scheme, Neighbourhood Watch was successful in bringing about a reduction not just in burglary but in all forms of major crime. This may reflect a degree of police involvement with citizens' concern about crime priorities which is less likely to occur in situations where the police are attempting to impose such schemes 'from above' and do not have a close relationship with the local community. The Home Office guide mentioned above gives voice to a certain contempt for the public when it comes to matters of crime:

For example, it could emerge that what concerns neighbours most and gives rise to most fear is unruly, uncivil behaviour, perhaps bordering on rowdyism and accompanied by vandalism. Yet the police may *know* that the most frequently occurring crime in the area is burglary and consequently feel that it is on that crime that attention and resources should be focused . . . If enthusiasm and support cannot be generated in the first instance towards police-defined problems, then it has been found useful to concentrate in the short term on residents' fears whilst continuing to seek support on other issues. Since fear can be as troublesome as crime itself the effects might well be beneficial. (Home Office 1984b, p. 2, our emphasis)

Such arrogance from state institutions with regard to definitions of public needs is by no means restricted to the police. But here it is particularly crass, for it is well known that burglary has an especially high reportage rate, for reasons of insurance, and that the reportage of other crimes is governed partly by the public's evaluation of the police. The notion of the police 'generating support' for issues that they 'know' more about than the public do – the public, who bear the brunt of crime – is a succinct statement of the case for greater local democratic accountability of police policy-making.

The other background factor to the success of the NWS in Detroit was pre-existing community organization. Again, transferring to the British situation, one can see some of the problems. Setting up NWSs in areas without any sense of community identity would be difficult in any case. Although crime rates are rising and the fear of crime is considerable, the actual experience of crime is widely dispersed, and the issue is not sufficiently high-profile to galvanize large numbers of people into going to a police-organized meeting and volunteering to be street coordinators in order to pass on observations from the street residents to the local police. 'Freda Applebaum, who has held the Fortess Road meetings in her flat, is disappointed that the circulation of more than 100 invitations attracted fewer than 20 positive replies. "People moan and groan about getting broken into but they are not very inclined to want to help themselves"' (*Hampstead and Highgate Express*, 25 November 1983).

The setting-up of NWSs in areas without a strong integrative community organization could exacerbate racial antagonism. Where a community has no sense of common purpose, nor understanding about needs and problems that cut across racial differences, then 'being on the lookout for suspicious happenings' can become very oppressive. The extent of racial prejudice in the police being what it is, the police can even find themselves adding fuel to the flames. A report of a police constable addressing the residents of Hampstead Garden Suburb on how NWSs could help to reduce burglary in the area illustrates the point: 'If you hear the sound of breaking glass and see a black man walking down the street with a bag, obviously you call the police' (*Hampstead and Highgate Express*, 7 October 1983). Such behaviour is only a step from vigilantism, which would have disastrous consequences. The police are very aware of this issue and of the need to discourage any identification of NWSs with citizens taking the law into their own hands. But the matter may not be entirely within their, the police's, hands. The very existence of NWSs in situations where the police are calling for greater public involvement in the fight against crime, albeit in a passive information-gathering role, and where there is a high level of racial prejudice with white racists blaming black youth for most of the area crime, is inevitably conducive to vigilantism.

What success have NWSs had in Britain so far? Information is as yet scarce, and what there is is not very reliable. In May 1985 there were over 200 schemes functioning in London listed by the Metropolitan Police. The only information as to their effectiveness was that contained in Sir Kenneth Newman's Press release of February 1984, which gave the statistics from just one scheme, in the Hurlingham area of Fulham. This scheme resulted in a 50 per cent reduction in burglary and a 52 per cent reduction in all major crime over the months of September and October 1984, and a further fall of 58 per cent in burglary and 42 per cent in all major crime during the November. It is of course very difficult to draw conclusions from a couple of months. Crime fluctuates throughout the year, and initial enthusiasm on the part of the public may taper off. But what is strange is that the large falls in crime (again, percentages – we are not told the actual figures) within the Neighbourhood Watch area were accompanied, at least in the September and October, by smaller but way above average reductions in crime for the Fulham division as a whole. Thus major crime fell in the Fulham division as a whole by 21 per cent over the first two months of the Hurlingham scheme, although it started to rise again, by 8 per cent, in November 1984. What may well have been the case here was that the police regarded the Hurlingham scheme as something of a showcase Neighbourhood Watch and diverted a lot of resources into the division in general, at least for the September and October. If they eased off in November, the increase in crime for the division as a whole might represent some displacement of crime from the Neighbourhood Watch area to the surrounding area. All this is of course conjectural, since no further information was given in the police Press release, which certainly regarded it as no part of the police's task to explain an extraordinarily high reduction in crime, by contrast with the London figures as a whole, for the areas surrounding the Hurlingham scheme.

In conclusion, it is worth emphasizing that community-based initiatives in crime prevention are, in themselves, an important innovation. What we have tried to stress, through the comparison of one American scheme with what is generally the case in Britain, is the importance of the accompanying background of police accountability and community organization. This seems to us a powerful reason why it should be, in the British context, a local authority rather than a police function to operate such schemes. We shall return to a fuller discussion of this in the final chapter.

6
The Problems of
Multi-Agency Policing

A significant element in the police response to the crisis has involved the development of a 'multi-agency' approach to problems of crime control. While pressure for the 'toughening up' of traditional police methods (many of the powers conferred by the Police and Criminal Evidence Act) has come largely from within the police forces, the articulation of the multi-agency philosophy has come from a battery of high-level think-tanks and police chiefs such as Sir Kenneth Newman at the Met, building upon the philosophy articulated over the previous decade by John Alderson, former Chief Constable of Devon and Cornwall.

The multi-agency approach involves two things: first, the shift in emphasis from crime detection and deterrence to crime prevention, with the aim of reducing the opportunities to commit crime; and second, the shifting of responsibility from the police alone to the cooperative framework of police plus other agencies in the social welfare field (local authority housing, social services and education), together with the local community itself. The impetus to adopt a multi-agency approach has not been simply the crisis in police–community relations revealed by the riots of 1981 and by Lord Scarman. A powerful additional factor has been the increasing public criticism of low clear-up rates for important categories of crime. This convinced many police chiefs that the reactive or 'fire brigade' style of policing, which developed during the sixties and seventies, needed to be modified and supplemented by an approach which reduced the opportunities for people to commit crime.

The problem with the thinking and with many of the initiatives currently behind multi-agency cooperation in crime prevention is the familiar one of important policy initiatives being taken under the guise of purely 'administrative' issues, and therefore in the absence of public debate concerning their wisdom or of opportunities for their scrutiny by the public. It will be a major argument of this chapter that the institution-alization of multi-agency policing, through the 'back door' of administrative planning within police (and Home Office) organization, will develop forms of cooperation between the police and other agencies which will both undermine some of the remaining democratic features of our society and fail to contain crime.

But it should not be thought that the intention of police innovators like Sir Kenneth Newman is directly to undermine democracy and combine the police with other agencies as part of a 'seamless web' of authoritarian political control. If this does occur it will be the unintended consequence of measures motivated, as we have seen, by a concern to deflect public criticism particularly of police clear-up rates – indeed, if anything, to diminish rather than extend the role of the police in the containment of crime. But it is the consequences that count. A diminution of police responsibility for crime control, in the context of increased powers of arrest and detention, entry to premises and seizure of documents, as well as stop and search, coupled with the general move on the part of a Tory government to reduce the local control of social planning agencies and of the police forces themselves, forms precisely the nexus of circumstances that will produce a fundamental shift towards an increasingly authoritarian style of policing impervious to public criticism.

The development of a multi-agency approach to the con-tainment of crime has, of course, required central government initiatives incorporating officials of other agencies besides the police forces. Up to 1981 inter-agency thinking on crime prevention had been primarily of the 'locks and bolts' variety. The Home Office had a standing committee on crime prevention which was, for example, instrumental in persuading motor manufacturers to fit steering-column locks on motor vehicles. But since 1981 rapid new developments have taken place. In 1982 Whitehall established an interdepartmental working group under Sir Brian Cubbon involving senior officials from the DHSS, the Department of the Environment, the Welsh and Scottish Offices and others. In September 1982 the group organized a four-day seminar at the police staff college at Bramshill, at which police and senior local government officials mingled to discuss crime prevention strategies and at which the police–local government interface was a major theme. The conference was followed by the issue to local authorities of a series of draft circulars during 1983 and 1984 embodying much of the thinking of the seminar.

In addition the Home Office, for its own distinct reasons, has become a major advocate of the multi-agency approach. In March 1983 the Home Office Interdepartmental Group on Crime wrote a report entitled *Crime Reduction*. This was followed in July 1983 by the establishment of a Home Office Crime Prevention Unit. *Crime Reduction* served to bring out both sides of the coin of the multi-agency approach. If policemen like Sir Kenneth Newman had been mainly focusing on the crime prevention role other agencies might take, a second theme – long advocated by the exponents of advanced forms of 'community policing' such as John Alderson when Chief Constable of Devon and Cornwall (and in his subsequent writings) – that the police should reciprocally extend their activities into spheres traditionally the preserve of other agencies, is now being placed firmly on the agenda: 'First there is a case for developing and broadening the role of the police in crime reduction . . . there is also a role for the police outside their traditional sphere: in local decision-making, for example, in the area of planning and environmental policies and in local activities such as schools and youth work' (Home Office 1983a).

Once more, fundamental issues concerning the relationship

between the police and the public are being discussed behind
closed doors without any genuine public discussion. Some of
the implications of this type of thinking in the working out of
actual policies and strategies will be explored in a moment.
Meanwhile, it is useful to understand the particular motivation
of the Home Office in its contributions to the debate on multi-
agency policing. The background to Home Office thinking is
the recently acquired view in these circles that as far as
policing is concerned, 'more of the same' will have diminishing
returns: 'In particular, it is becoming clear that the effectiveness of the "core" of policing – preventative patrol and
criminal investigation – cannot be significantly improved by
increased manning levels. Certainly, "saturation" patrolling
may achieve short-term reductions in crime but only at very
heavy cost – both financial and in terms of relations between
police and public' (Home Office 1983a). This particular
conclusion was justified by the Home Office in its reference to
a review of recent criminological research: 'findings now to
hand suggest that at present the development of situational
prevention affords the best prospect for the reduction of
crime.' In other words, an emphasis on crime prevention
involving other agencies besides the police is another conclusion to be drawn from the analysis we discussed in Chapter 3.
If more police are going to make little difference to crime
control, then of course inter-agency crime prevention makes
immediate policy sense.

It should be clear from what has been said so far that the
response by the police and by government agencies to the
crisis in crime control has not been coherent. Certainly, there is
little real evidence to believe that an overall strategy exists
which 'merges at the local level the coercive and consensual
functions of government enabling the police to wield a frightening mixture of repressive powers, on the one hand, and
programmes of social intervention on the other, as mutually
reinforcing tools in their efforts to control and contain the
political struggles of the black and working-class communities'
(Bridges 1982, p. 25).

It is worth spelling out how we diverge from such an analysis. First, the main impetus for changes in policing strategy has come from the crisis in crime control, the day-to-day work of the police. This, as we argued in the first part of this book, has produced the overwhelming pressure for change. This is evident both in Sir Kenneth Newman's concern with crime clear-up rates and in the Home Office's discovery of the law of diminishing returns. Neither is concerned in the first instance with the problem of 'how to contain the political struggles of the black and working-class communities'. Nor did the extension of police powers of arrest, detention, stop and search, and so on, contained in the Police and Criminal Evidence Act, originate directly from 'the class struggle'. As Baldwin and Kinsey (1982) have shown, the origin of much of that legislation lay in organized police representation to the Royal Commission on Criminal Procedure, which recommended the legalization of *de facto* police practices such as extended interrogation and unlawful detention which, again, were primarily concerned with extracting confessions from individuals suspected of having committed 'ordinary' crimes.

However, the fact that the origin of the new police powers and strategies such as multi-agency cooperation lies in the problems of combating crime rather than in an overtly political concern with containing class struggle, does not mean that such changes are not a threat to civil liberties. Nor does it imply that changes originating from the response to the problem of crime containment will not be recruited to the service of more repressive political concerns. This is so for a number of obvious reasons. Government and mass media may seek to criminalize hitherto legitimate industrial relations matters, such as organized picketing by strikers. Techniques such as computer storage and retrieval of 'criminal intelligence' may be easily diverted to the tasks of political surveillance. Indeed, we can discern a reverse process whereby initiatives in police tactics arising out of political class confrontations may be fed back into the day-to-day activities of crime control. It is very likely that the lessons learned by police forces in the realm of inter-force cooperation during the miners' strike will become permanent fixtures of policing in the United Kingdom. All we are claiming is that the types of changes we are discussing in this book have originated primarily as attempts to respond to what is perceived as, and is in fact, a crisis in the ability of the police to control crime.

But, perhaps more important, in contrast to writers such as Lee Bridges, we do not see these measures as coherent. We do not see the proposals for multi-agency cooperation between police and welfare agencies and local authorities on the one hand, and the extended police powers in the field of 'normal' police work as contained in the Police and Criminal Evidence Act on the other, as a structure of 'mutually reinforcing tools'. What we are concerned to argue, and to which we shall now move, is that these measures are internally contradictory and will not solve the problems of crime. And furthermore, we link their failure to solve the problems of crime precisely with their being a threat to civil liberties. No system of authoritarian policing will solve the problem of crime control.

Varieties of Multi-Agency Policing

Hitherto we have defined multi-agency policing, in very general terms, as the close cooperation between police and local education, housing, and social work agencies, together with the general public, in the implementation of strategies aimed at crime prevention. A closer look at the types of initiatives which are either emerging or being talked about – some have been around a long time and others are still in the heads of planners – reveals a number of different relationships between other agencies and the police. A rough classification of these will perhaps enable us to see more clearly the origins of some of the contradictions and problems which, in our opinion, multi-agency policing as a form of crime control will encounter.

Separate and Equal

Different agencies, working quite independently of one another, may include crime prevention as an aspect of their
normal functioning. This, the weakest form of what is now
called multi-agency cooperation, has been around for a long
time, and it generally enables other agencies to make their
contribution with only a minimal contact with the police.
Examples come readily from the housing field. In 1981
Merseyside police, in conjunction with the regional office of
the Housing Corporation and the Merseyside Voluntary
Housing Group, published *Secure Homes: A Guide to Specification
in the Design of Dwellings*. In 1982 the Technical Policy Division
of the Greater London Council produced, in consultation with
Scotland Yard, a design guide entitled *Security in Housing Blocks
– Phone Entry Systems*. Whether such manuals are produced by
the police or by housing authorities makes little difference:
multi-agency cooperation is simply an exchange of technical
information to enable local government or even private housing bodies to secure their property. All that has really changed
in this area is the importation of new terminology with a more
grandiose military connotation, such as 'target-hardening'.
The designated activities may extend into the owner-occupier
sector or become the basis for new forms of contact between
the police and individual members of the public. Recently, for
example, police forces have been engaging in a leaflet campaign
to encourage residents to mark their household property with
invisible ink. Here again, the role of the police in the
relationship is primarily that of technical adviser.

It becomes clear that many of the forms of 'multi-agency'
cooperation in crime prevention are mundane and traditional.
We can, however, expect to see here a more organized police
involvement, branching away from the traditional areas of
advice on 'target-hardening'. We have already quoted the
Home Office's enthusiasm for the increased involvement of
police 'in the area of planning and environmental policies'.

Housing authorities are embracing a new jargon involving terms such as 'natural surveillance' and 'defensible space'. Such concepts go beyond the securing of individual homes by means of locks and entry-phones, to the design of housing estates that can minimize the opportunities for young people to gather together to plan or execute vandalism or other mischief out of sight of adult residents.

In a similar vein, much social work and youth work can be considered as forms of crime prevention pursued quite independently of the police. Whatever the kind and frequency of contact between youth workers and the police, for all sorts of reasons concerning the activities of young people, the very act of attempting to establish youth clubs and centres to get youngsters off the streets and away from situations which may lead them into crime is of itself a crime-prevention activity. Youth workers may work in conjunction with other non-police agencies, such as local authority housing departments, tenants' associations and voluntary sector bodies like the National Association for the Care and Resettlement of Offenders (NACRO) or the National Association of Youth Clubs (NAYC), in an attempt to organize activities to keep kids 'out of trouble' on particular housing estates. Again, in this general sense there is a lot of 'multi-agency policing', and it has been going on for some time, much of it with minimal police input. What involvement there is, is by virtue of the fact that the police have traditionally made it their business to know what goes on in a locality and to develop informal liaison with a wide variety of people who know the area and are therefore to be seen as potential sources of criminal intelligence.

But – and this is the key point – the crime prevention activities of social work agencies and housing departments can be considered as an aspect of the normal working of such agencies, and do not *per se* involve a relationship with the police that compromises the independence of the agency to carry out its policies and tasks as it sees fit. It may 'buy in' technical information on crime prevention from the police, but this is quite different from allowing the police any decision-making role that could influence the working of the agency. As we have noted, this is precisely what starts to happen if police become, as the Home Office urges, more closely involved in planning and environmental design activities: they gain the opportunity to influence the decision-making process within the agency itself by actually participating in it. This is the hallmark of the second type of multi-agency cooperation, involving joint action.

Joint Action

A much stronger form of multi-agency policing involves the police and other agencies in a new working relationship. Police and social service agencies may combine to produce a joint strategy against crime of a particular type (for example, vandalism by young people) or in a particular area such as a housing estate. This may result in the setting-up of new joint institutions and in new levels of information-sharing mutual access to records and other data.

The Bramshill seminar, referred to earlier, was clear about the potential of much closer information-exchange between the police and other agencies in the sphere of crime prevention:

Many local agencies have some data about the pattern and nature of juvenile offending in the area: this information needs to be pooled and analysed as a preliminary to effective joint action. The police, for example, can from their records plot the particular areas or estates from which apprehended offenders come. Similarly, information about children excluded or truanting from schools can be presented systematically. Social services case loads can be plotted according to district. In fact it is often possible to determine those localities within a given area where action is most needed and the information provided will often suggest the form that action might take. (Bramshill 1982, p. 19)

In seeking to translate these guidelines into a set of strategies for local authorities, the 1983 *Draft Circular on Crime Prevention* to local authorities was at pains to emphasize that 'It is the

collection and collation of aggregate data that is being suggested and *not* information about identifiable individuals: and
this circular is *not* intended to alter or extend in any way
agencies for the exchange of confidential information' (Home
Office 1983b, para. 9, original emphasis). Moreover, the
circular continued, the flow of information should not be
considered as one-way only, from local authority agencies to
the police:

The police are an obvious major source of data, and local authorities
would be helped if the police were to make available to them
information on local patterns of crime which describe the characteristics of specific crimes. There are also many other sources besides
the police, such as insurance companies . . . the Post Office and the
Gas and Electricity Boards when damage to their property is
involved. Local Authority departments in particular are likely to be
rich sources both of information directly about crime, such as
vandalism of school buildings or racial attacks on multi-ethnic
housing estates, and of the social and demographic data necessary to
place crime in its local context. Such data might for example include
information about housing stock, population characteristics and
perhaps transport and recreational facilities in areas noted for high
levels of crime and disorder. (para. 10)

So what is envisaged is a general opening up of the agencies in
order to share aggregate data and to formulate joint strategies
for crime prevention. Some of the practical implications of
such extensive data-sharing can be glimpsed in Sir Kenneth
Newman's plan to institute the development of neighbourhood computer profiles. At present the Met is engaged in
research under the guise of a neighbourhood policing project
which

involves research into the problem of urban policing and the
availability and deployment of police resources. This research is
directed towards the development and evaluation of a system of
policing within a given area which is responsive to local needs and
which enables the police to identify and prevent problems . . . It is
envisaged that the scheme will include a locally based computerised

information system for the use of patrolling officers and station management and a training programme to familiarise officers with the elements described. (Newman 1983, p. 36)

In the housing field the Department of the Environment's Priority Estates project offers an example of joint action by agencies in crime prevention. After 1978, when the initial research was completed, several local authorities responded to the call for initiatives on difficult-to-let estates where crime and vandalism combined with physical deterioration to reduce their attractiveness to potential tenants. As the Bramshill seminar reported, joint action was a crucial part of the strategy:

It became apparent that other agencies needed to make a contribution to the well-being of the estates, in particular, the police. Some caretaking security was required and over the past few years cooperation with the police has become of prime importance in the improvement of estate security. Several local authority schemes now include community police in their estate teams. (Bramshill 1982, p. 8)

In addition to the involvement of police at a local level in estate security, local tenants' associations have themselves been encouraged to play an active part. The Housing Services Advisory Group on council estate security recommended that 'authorities should help and encourage tenants' associations and other groups to play their part in safeguarding and improving the environment and to assist in identifying problems as they occurred' (Bramshill 1982, p. 10).

In the social services field, a major initiative in multi-agency work has centered on the area of juvenile offenders. A project is currently being carried out by the juvenile crime unit of NACRO, to devise methods of inter-agency cooperation to deal with juvenile crime. The thinking in this area has grown out of the development of 'intermediate treatment', the activities of police juvenile bureaux and the practice of cautioning young offenders. The basic philosophy has been to devise ways of keeping young people who do commit offences out of the court system.

One of the most successful and interesting innovations along these lines has taken place in Northamptonshire. Schemes recently established in Corby and Wellingborough involve an agreement by the chief inspector of police to submit every juvenile case to a bureau for consideration. The bureau team consists of five people, a chairperson and four others seconded from different agencies – police, social services, probation, education – and the police undertake to accept the recommendations of the bureau unless there appear to be compelling reasons why not to do so. Bureau recommendations include counselling and apology by offenders to their victims. A feature of the scheme is the strong support from the local police. Speaking at a conference in Birmingham, Maurice Buck, the chief constable of the Northamptonshire force, expressed his belief that 'the coordinated inter-agency approach is more likely to enhance the quality of decision-making' reflected in the juvenile liaison bureau recommendations. He affirmed that 'prevention is the cornerstone of police activity in Northamptonshire' (Buck et al. 1983).

The Northamptonshire experiment is the most ambitious, but the Bramshill seminar reported the existence of similar initiatives in Exeter and Doncaster. Of course, as the seminar made clear, the possibility of joint action rests with the decision of the police to participate, since 'it is the police who have responsibility for deciding which young offenders should appear before the courts . . . The decision must remain theirs in each individual case, but the machinery enables them to discharge their responsibility in the light of all the information available for each particular youngster' (Bramshill 1982, p. 15).

By far the most ambitious initiatives in multi-agency policing in the area of joint action concern the relationship between the police and the public itself. The Police and Criminal Evidence Act 1984 makes a statutory requirement of what is at present a blossoming initiative in some areas: police–

community liaison panels. Sir Kenneth Newman has given great emphasis to the role of police–community liaison in constructing area policing plans and identifying the specific policing needs of each area:

I see consultative committees as the focal point for my attempts to encourage a problem-solving approach to many of the issues which have hitherto been dealt with exclusively by police but which are suitable for more broadly based community action. For example, initiatives to combat juvenile delinquency and vandalism must involve other social agencies, parents and teachers as well as the police. Our experience with the Lambeth Community/Police consultative group also encourages me to believe that the committees will help police achieve some consensus about the optimum style and method of policing for different areas . . . My aim is that this planning framework should enable the Force to work with the public with a view to achieving shared objectives based on mutual understanding and consensus about strategy. (Newman 1983, p. 4)

The central conception here is important. The 'public' is not being thought of simply as a source of *demands* – for a particular type of policing policy, for example‾ but as an *agency* in its own right alongside social services, education and so on, which can take positive steps, in conjunction with the police, to solve crime. This view is found also in the Bramshill seminar:

the post-Scarman consultative arrangements were seen to provide a most valuable forum for discussion on crime prevention matters, *provided* they offered a genuine channel of understanding in both directions. On this point there was consensus: it was of equal importance that – as a result of consultation – the police were themselves informed of the wishes of the community, and at the same time that the community was left in no doubt as to its responsibility for crime reduction and the contribution it could make to it. (Bramshill 1982, p. 28)

The seminar linked the conception of the public as a source of demands on the police with the conception of the public as an agency to work alongside the police: 'Participants were convinced that public participation would not be increased where the police and local authorities continued to entertain, and act on, misconceptions about community needs. The case for carrying out local surveys – which would form the basis for collaborative crime prevention initiatives – was strongly presented' (p. 28).

So policing policy can be made to correspond with public demands through the consultation process, and as a result the public will be willing to cooperate in joint action with the police as a crime-prevention agency in its own right. Parents taking more responsibility for what their teenage children do in the evenings is an obvious example. Self-policing is particularly appropriate on public occasions: football clubs taking more responsibility for their supporters as a way of combating football violence, for instance. The Bramshill discussion was, of course, aware that 'seeking public involvement may give rise to excesses, notably the formation of vigilante groups.' However, participants pointed to initiatives which had successfully avoided such problems, and concluded that they should not be allowed to deter efforts to enlist public support. The danger of vigilantism is, however, ever present, and while police rhetoric has sometimes stressed the role of the public as an agency engaging in joint action with the police, in practice the 'joint' element is restricted to the 'two-way consultation' whereby policing policy will be made to correspond with public demands, and where the public are to take to the field with an active role in crime prevention it is to be under the firm control of the police. At this point it is appropriate to turn to the final type of multi-agency policing, in which, again, the other agencies remain under the firm direction of the police.

Colonization

This last type of multi-agency policing involves other institutions in the crime-prevention or, on occasions, detection, process essentially as appendages of the police. To the extent that they do become involved, they remain passive providers of information to the police, or take what positive action they may be able to under firm police control. Colonization may involve quite simple activities: for example, the Criminal Investigation Department, with the agreement of local authority housing departments, uses flats for surveillance purposes. This is a well established practice. But by far the most important initiatives of this type are the Neighbourhood Watch schemes discussed in the previous chapter. One aspect of their work – the transmission of information to the police concerning 'suspicious circumstances' – is an example of the colonization of the public as an auxiliary information-gathering organ of the police.

Some Problems of Multi-Agency Policing

Many of the strategies that we have described above are not new. Other elements, though, are very new: perhaps most important of all is the elevation of crime prevention to the all-embracing philosophy of multi-agency policing, now regarded as a central arm of policing in the modern city. Some considerable time will have to elapse before many of the problems become clear, and by then, of course, it may be too late to alter the course of events. So it is of crucial importance to think ahead and try to draw out, in the form of hypotheses, some of the *likely* problems with such policies. Any policy can attempt, in its early stages, to defend itself from criticism on the grounds that it is 'too early to tell' and that the scheme should be 'given a chance to work'. Our standpoint in this book is rather that there are quite fundamental issues at stake which need to be considered now, and that steps must be taken as soon as possible, as part of a socialist policing policy, to make sure that some of the predictions which will be made below do not become a reality.

The first problem that characterizes the multi-agency approach to policing is one inherent in any strategy of situational crime prevention – that of threat to freedom. Ron Clarke, one of the leading advocates in Home Office circles of preventive approaches to crime, is aware of the problems:

Many members of the general public might . . . find it objectionable that crime was being stopped, not by punishing wrong-doers, but by inconveniencing the law-abiding. The fact that opportunity-reducing and risk-increasing measures are too readily identified with their more unattractive aspects (barbed wire, heavy padlocks, guard dogs and private security forces) adds fuel to the fire. And in some of their more sophisticated forms (closed circuit television surveillance and electronic intruder alarms) they provoke fears on the one hand of 'big brother' forms of state control and on the other of a 'fortress society' in which citizens in perpetual fear of their fellows scuttle from one fortified environment to another. (Clarke 1980, pp. 136–47)

These comments apply most readily to those areas of the multi-agency approach which involve the tactics of 'target-hardening' and 'designing out crime' (that is, designing homes in such a way as to exclude crime) adopted in housing schemes. The fact that the police may be increasingly involved in the planning of these schemes is less important than the impact of such innovations on people's freedom. Even where police are not involved, elaborate approaches to crime prevention may constrict freedom of action. Socialists, and all those concerned with protecting individual freedom, should therefore be very wary of any form of situational crime prevention. This is not to say that a preventive approach can play no part in a socialist criminal policy: rather, that we must be aware of, and avoid, two tendencies. The first is what might be called 'social behaviourism': the idea that human behaviour is purely and simply a product of the structures and opportunities within which it takes place. The second is the displacement of politics by technology in which important areas of social policy – and crime prevention is one such – become defined as technical management problems rather than problems to be resolved by political argument and compromise between different social groups.

'Social behaviourism' can lead to an exaggerated belief in the efficiency of prevention measures. The law of diminishing returns as applied to the relation between crime rates and police manpower has been, as we have noted, recently discovered in Home Office circles, and has become a reason for shifting emphasis in the direction of crime prevention. But the law of diminishing returns can also apply to preventive measures themselves. Beyond a certain point, increases in such measures as 'target-hardening' and 'natural surveillance' will have marginal effects in further reducing crime, yet markedly increase the apprehension of innocent citizens and restrict their free social space. Regimes of barbed wire, searchlights and watch towers on housing estates would have such an effect. Bearing in mind that prisons are probably the most elaborate situational crime-prevention systems, yet have a high rate of rule infringement by inmates, the effectiveness of all but the most elementary preventive precautions is called into doubt. Individuals are not simply the product of the structures that surround them.

Such measures will, moreover, tend to be maximally oppressive to the liberties of innocent persons, if they are devised from above by planners and technocrats, including the police, rather than arising out of a process of political debate and compromise between groups in the community whose interests will be affected. Such a debate, of course, presupposes a democratic participatory system of local government. One obvious conflict of interests would be that between adult residents of housing estates concerned to reduce noise and minimize the opportunities for vandalism and burglary on the one hand, and young people needing free space away from the surveillance of adults yet close to home in which they can meet and play. With crime-prevention strategies, the deterrence of the potential individual offender through the certainty of detection by police, aided by a flow of public information, is replaced by the removal of the opportunity for *anyone* to act in certain ways or to escape from public surveillance: obviously this raises questions concerning the interests and needs of the

wider community, and not just of the groups whose vulnerability to crime is being reduced by the measures.

   The second tendency concerns the inherent instability built
into the relationship between the police and other agencies in
any cooperative enterprise in the field of crime prevention,
whereby in whichever of the three styles of multi-agency
cooperation outlined above an initiative may begin, there will
be pressures of 'drift' in the direction of the third type:
colonization of the other agency by the police. The result will
be the recruitment of other agencies as surrogates to the
police, and a weakening of their capacity to operate independently. This widening of the net of policing will come about
not as a result of an articulated policy of dismantlement of the
democratic state and its welfare agencies, but as the result of a
drift originating at ground level in the day-to-day relations of
cooperation between agencies, all of whom start off with
different methods of operating and forms of accountability to
the public, as well as elements of role conflict with one another
in their normal modes of operation. There are two main
pressures that can be foreseen as the driving force of the 'drift'
to colonization'. First, the agencies which have no element of
accountability to the local community, or a very weak one (for
example, the police), will tend to act as an *external* constraint
upon the democratic operation of those agencies which do
have some sort of accountability to the local community.
Second, that close cooperation with 'non-accountable' agencies,
the police in particular, will undermine *from within* the capacity
of other agencies to act independently, not only in the area of
crime prevention but also in other areas more normally
considered to be their province. We shall discuss these in turn.

External Constraints

Any agency may reject the advice of any other. But when close
cooperation between agencies is established in the field of
crime prevention – and when crime prevention has a high
public priority – then it will be difficult for other agencies to

reject the advice of the police where the latter can establish that law and order issues are at stake. Consider the following example. A local housing authority, in accordance with the political priorities established by local government, desires to allocate housing on a new or renovated estate to ethnic-minority families. Few ethnic-minority families have hitherto settled on the estate and there is likely to be some opposition from certain groups of existing tenants and from right-wing extremist political groups in the area. The police may liaise with the housing authority, advising them that a 'law and order problem' is likely to result from such an allocation policy and therefore the council should think again. The police cannot, of course, force the council to change its policy, but in the context of close cooperation in crime prevention on housing estates the advice of the police will have to be taken very seriously. It is not being suggested that the police would automatically give such advice in such a situation. Local commanders might say to the council, 'Tell us the estates on which new housing is going to be allocated to ethnic minorities, and we'll keep a special eye on the area and check up on the activities of local right-wing extremists.' But the point is that the almost total lack of accountability of police policy-making to the local community will mean that the political process which determines council policy will have little impact on the police, except by accident. Whichever line the police took on the issue would not be a result of any political discourse; it would be arbitrary. On this particular policy, resistance might well come from other quarters: from elements in the local tenants' association, for example. However, the resolution of such conflicts will be part of the local political process. The point is that the police will stand outside that process, but nonetheless the actual policies they pursue may act as a constraint on that process, and upon the freedom of action of agencies answerable to it.

Metropolitan Police policy on racial harassment has, until very recently, been quite ambiguous. A Home Office study on the incidence of racial attacks published in November 1981 argued that 'For the police, the problem of racial attacks is necessarily only one particular manifestation of crime. It cannot claim an automatic priority. But there was, nonetheless, a tendency on the part of the police to underestimate the significance of racialist incidents and activities for those attacked or threatened' (Home Office 1981, para. 76). An investigation into racial harassment by the Greater London Council which took evidence from a wide variety of groups, individuals and local London boroughs concluded that the relations between local authority housing departments and the police was haphazard:

Evidence from local authority housing departments confirmed the views of other witnesses that the response of the police was generally inadequate. While there were some 'exceptionally good' individual officers, the failure of the police to respond quickly to incidents and their reluctance to prosecute meant that the police response was often totally ineffective. The position of the home beat officer was also equivocal. They could be removed at short notice for policing duties elsewhere (for example, to demonstrations), and there was no guarantee that a good officer would be retained for any length of time. (GLC 1983, p. 104)

After the publication of the Home Office report on racial attacks, the Metropolitan Police announced a widening of the scope of racial incidents recorded – all incidents were to be recorded irrespective of whether an offence had been committed. The definition of whether an incident had a racial motive was to be widened, to include the victims' perception as well as that of the police. These changes resulted in a sharp increase in the number of racial incidents recorded, nearly doubling after the new procedures were introduced in May 1982. More recently, in January 1985 Sir Kenneth Newman, the Metropolitan Police Commissioner, announced that along with vandalism and drug abuse racial attackes were to be added to the crime-fighting priorities of London's police. What the issue of racial attacks in London illustrates is that police policy-making can move in the right directions – what happens on the ground is, of course, a different matter – but it is clear that local authority housing departments, which in many boroughs have been concerned about the question of racial attacks for some considerable time, have no direct influence on police policy-making one way or the other. A local authority responsibility not only for housing but also for policing could have established a long time ago a clear, coordinated policy in accordance with the general wishes of the electorate.

An analogous situation may arise in the case of increased cooperation between social work agencies and the police, particularly in the field of juvenile diversion (non-custodial approaches to juvenile justice). Social work agencies find themselves involved in close cooperation with the police in juvenile diversion, for which the framework of cautioning procedure is entirely beyond their control. There is some evidence, for example (Landau 1981; Pitts 1979), that police cautioning procedures discriminate against black youngsters, who get a disproportionate number of custodial sentences. Social work agencies may wish to change this type of policy at a local level, but the police may be unwilling to contemplate change. Again, the lack of accountability in police policy formation acts as an external constraint on social workers. Any change that does occur, or, indeed, the parameters of cautioning policy *per se*, will be arrived at by, at the best, a process of informal inter-agency bargaining.

But there is, apart from these specific examples, a general trend at work in current conceptions of multi-agency policing which would take inter-agency coordination out of the democratic level of local government entirely. The Bramshill seminar ruminated about where the responsibility for co-ordination should lie:

Such a task could fall to the police authorities since they include amongst their membership representatives of a number of local interests, and will no doubt have a significant part to play in post-Scarman consultative arrangements. Alternatively, and especially in view of the need for close interdepartmental collaboration between community services, there is a strong argument for placing primary responsibility on the shoulders of the chief executive. (Bramshill 1982, p. 34)

Here the requirements of pluralistic democracy and the exigencies of technical coordination are nicely juxtaposed. The Home Office *Draft Circular on Crime Prevention* attempted an amalgamation by suggesting a three-stage process. First:

So far as local authorities are concerned, the way forward here might be to identify individuals (initially, perhaps, at chief officer/director level) within the authority to whom the development of a crime prevention dimension in policies and procedures would fall . . . it is likely that, at a minimum, the police, the magistracy, the social and probation services and the departments of education, housing and highways will all need to be involved, as will those responsible for planning and environment and the provision of leisure facilities. (Home Office 1983b, para. 21)

Second:

These official 'core' meetings might be linked with other regular discussions designed to bring in commuity and voluntary groups, the churches, and representatives of local industrial, business and commercial concerns. In urban areas where there are inner-city partnerships or programme arrangements these should be part of the consultation process. (para. 21)

Finally, once a local crime-prevention plan has emerged out of discussion at these two levels, 'its implementation should be endorsed both by local elected representatives and relevant local government departments and agencies including the police' (para. 22).

There are two things to note about this conception of the local multi-agency policing coordination process. First, it puts us firmly into the tradition of a 'local corporatism' in which, in the first instance, the whole formulation of the problems is to be seen as a technical matter for local experts, the 'core group'. Then, once a perspective has been formulated, significant interests in the locality can be sounded out. And then, presumably when the plan has taken shape, it can be 'endorsed' by the local democratic process as *one among several* agencies whose approval must be secured. Any notion of democratic legitimacy or the need for the agreement of the majority of the electorate to such a plan, let alone its participation in plan formation at councillor level, is firmly buried among a welter of technical discourse by experts and consultation with significant interests. Interest consultation is an important part of the democratic process, but it must be under the overriding supremacy of the proper electoral process of political democracy. The notion that the local elected representatives of the people are simply one agency among many is firmly in keeping with current attacks on the legitimacy of local government.

The second notable aspect of this thinking is the overriding role of the police. Unlike most elements of the community, whether described as significant interests or as elected representatives who enter into the planning process once (at either the second or the third stage, as described above), the police and other local government agencies enter into the process twice, at stages one *and* three: that is, they are part of the core group which formulates the plan, and then they are among the agencies who are called upon to endorse it. Of all the agencies in this position, the police are at the focal point. Not only are they present both at plan formulation and endorsement stages, but in addition they will have access to a parallel structure of police–community liaison committees and will be conducting their own social surveys of public attitudes to crime and, presumably, crime prevention. This parallel consultation process has its own problems, as we shall see presently, but its main effect will be to make the police by far the strongest agency in the whole plan formation and endorsement process. The police will define the situation and the parameters of the debate for other agencies, and for the public itself. We shall discuss an alternative, more democratic, structure later. But we can remark here that the obvious necessary counter to such proposals as those surveyed above is to make the democratic process the central agency in plan formation and endorsement. The core group should consist of member-led subcommittees of the local council. Officers of agencies with a crime-prevention interest, including the police, can then give advice; particular interests in the community can be consulted through liaison panels and the final plan can be re-endorsed by full council. The local authority itself should take full control of all community liaison and any social surveys that are to be conducted.

Internal Constraints

It is important to understand that although multi-agency policing has become an important new addition to policing strategy, it is not, nor is it likely to become, the predominant form of policing. The Scarman Report stated clearly that existing strategies of 'hard' policing have to continue alongside the newer methods. 'Hard policing,' he reiterated, 'is often necessary . . . it requires the use on the streets of stop and search powers and of the occasional "saturation" operation' (Scarman 1981, para. 4.75). As we have noted, such methods are minimally effective in containing crime and maximally effective in alienating from the police precisely that section of the public which has most information about crime. Yet these are precisely the aspects of policing that have been strengthened by many of the provisions of the Police and Criminal Evidence Act, which make it easier, for example, for the police to set up road blocks or detain individuals.

Therefore, close cooperation with the police by other agencies and sections of the public has to be seen in a context in which 'hard' policing is on the increase and, with it, a growing alienation of vulnerable sections of the public from the police. The role adopted by the police in the 1984–5 strike by the National Union of Mineworkers resulted in a massive alienation from the police of sections of the traditional working-class community on whom they have been accustomed to look for support and cooperation. In July 1984 the Chief Constable of West Yorkshire made a 'plea from the heart' that the mining dispute end, and the sooner the better. According to the *Guardian*, 'He was worried about the period of rehabilitation that will have to take place in the mining communities . . . Policing the dispute was having an effect on his men and community policing had nearly come to a full stop because of lack of manpower' (26 July 1984).

The miners' strike raised a whole host of issues concerning the role of the police in industrial disputes, the development of a *de facto* national police force, the relationship between police authorities and chief constables, and many others. Some of them are discussed elsewhere in this book. The point here is that the use of the police in an overtly political role in containing a major industrial dispute, where both government and media redefined a matter of industrial relations as a matter of 'law and order', will undoubtedly have a major impact on the ability of the police to pursue strategies of community policing and inter-agency cooperation. The chief constable of West Yorkshire's worry that a period of rehabilitation would be necessary after the dispute was over is an admission that relations between police and community in a very traditional working-class area have reached a low ebb. What incentive is there, where there exists real bitterness between miners and their families and the police – and memories in mining communities are long – for local teachers, local government councillors and officials and the local community itself to get involved in new multi-agency initiatives? It is not that the use of the police as a weapon against the trade union movement by the Thatcher government is all part of a coherent plan of which multi-agency policing is the 'soft' component: on the contrary, the deterioration of police–community relations resulting from such political uses of the police will make many aspects of multi-agency policing impossible to effectively carry out. And it is not just a question of the episodic role of the police in industrial relations. The strengthening of police stop and search powers under the Police and Criminal Evidence Act will have similar consequences in reducing community willingness to cooperate in such initiatives. A general hostitility to the police will make the work of other agencies very difficult, if they are seen to be in close cooperation with the police.

For example, if youth workers cooperate closely with the police – in data-sharing, in jointly identifying problem estates and attempting to develop projects on them – and it becomes widely known among young people, then encounters by young people with 'hard' policing may alienate them from youth workers. Young people will not make the distinction between 'soft' multi-agency policing and 'hard' policing involving street stop and search operations and the like. They will simply see youth workers as in league with an oppressive police force. Likewise with social work in general, close cooperation with the police, data-sharing, identifying problem areas of the city, participating in joint liaison bureaux – even the exchange of personnel between police and social services, a process which has existed on a small scale in many localities for some time – may undermine the effectiveness of social workers on those occasions when they have to act *against* the police in defence of clients, particularly in court. This possible undermining of the 'separation of powers' between agencies involved in social control is a crucial aspect of multi-agency policing which will receive further consideration below.

In other areas of multi-agency policing a close cooperation with the police may undermine the effectiveness of bodies to act on their own account. Thus according to the GLC panel on vandalism (1984), one problem with close liaison with tenants' association representatives and community police on a housing estate in Brixton was that 'Tenants' association members had to be careful in their meetings with the police that they were "not seen as spies for the police". This was one of the fears and worries' (para. 73).

But perhaps the most important example of the deleterious effects of close cooperation with the police will be felt by the public itself. As we have seen, the establishment of community–police liaison on a working basis is an integral part of current thinking on multi-agency policing. The question that many discussions tend to ignore is what *is* the community? There tends to be an assumption that the community is there waiting to liaise with the police or any other agency. The notion of the community existing independently of the forms of communication that it establishes both internally and externally is a dangerous one. It leads easily to a 'culturalist' notion of community, which can be very divisive in the context of the ethnic and cultural plurality of the city today. Thus, in thinking about the dynamics of new forms of police–community liaison, we have to bear firmly in mind as a starting-point that the maximization of communication is one of the prerequisites for the existence of a community. It therefore follows that forms of communication which are distorted or one-sided may increase divisive tendencies.

When we consider the nature of current proposals for police–community liaison, several features stand out. First, the result of any such communication and discussion on the nature of crime will be synthesized and coordinated by the police. Sir Kenneth Newman's philosophy of police–community discussion is profoundly bureaucratic:

My preliminary thoughts are that each of the 75 Metropolitan Police divisions will formulate a divisional plan taking account of the views of the law-abiding community. These plans will be aggregated at the 24 districts, at which level the police commander will work closely with borough-based consultative committees in order to round out and finalise the district plans. The district plans will then be aggregated at each of the four Metropolitan areas under the command of deputy assistant commissioners, and finally from areas to force headquarters level. At headquarters the plans will be analysed to establish the requisite assistance for the support and facilitation of district and divisional plans. In this way it is intended that the whole Metropolitan Police organisation will be made responsive to local needs. (Newman 1983, p. 4)

The essence of this thinking is that the consultation process is simply the gathering and sifting of opinions, the synthesis of which is a technical issue that can be safely left in the hands of a bureaucracy. Completely absent is any recognition that what constitutes the community in the first place is a process of democratic political discussion of social problems, and that the focus for the formulation of policy must be the community itself and not the police bureaucracy. The implication of such an understanding is, of course, a proper system of police accountability at local level, but this is not our concern at the present time. Rather, it is that in the absence of such accountability, police–community liaison will simply be a question of the police gathering 'views' from the 'law-abiding community', which will then be bureaucratically synthesized. There is no recognition of the importance of the democratic process whereby the community chooses its representatives. The 'law-abiding community' is taken just as a collection of interests and views to be consulted. How will they be represented on the liaison committees?

Finally, if the consultation process is seen simply as a matter of collecting views rather than as a process of *debate* and the accountability of policy to that debate, then the representation of interests as a method of recording views can easily be supplemented or even replaced by social survey methods; and a feature of current police schemes is that local surveys of attitudes to the police and other 'market research' techniques exist alongside liaison panels. A democratic system of debate about policing policy might well use social surveys as a method of constituting an agenda, but would realize that opinions on issues change as a result of the process of debate itself. But where the synthesis of views is brought about not by democratic debate but by a bureaucratic process, social survey results may enter into plan formation alongside or, worse still, displace the results of dialogue.

The end result, then, of community–police liaison may well be – rather than a process of open democratic debate around public policy formation and accountability, out of which can arise a system of compromises and consensus about the policing needs of an area – a contrary process of accentuation of divisions and community conflicts. How will the representatives on police–community liaison panels be chosen? As there is no public control of policing policy, the democratic election to such panels will certainly not result in a large turnout of voters. People have little incentive to participate in a process over which they have little control. Whose interests are actually represented on the liaison panels may therefore well depend on which sectional interest of the community is most well organized or most prepared to spend the time. Articulate groups such as the white male middle class or extremist organizations may acquire a high profile. The poor and disorganized, with a tradition of hostility towards bureaucratic local state agencies and the police in particular, may be very difficult to mobilize. On some of the worst housing estates, for example, where crime is high and there is very little sense of local community, it may be extremely difficult to secure participation – particularly where there is no clearly visible link between participation and planning outcome. Furthermore, the police are not like a local council: they have neither the incentive nor the ability to mobilize participation. On the contrary, the norms and traditions of the police service may make it very difficult for officers at a local level to participate in anything that resembles a 'debate', within even restricted sections of local communities. As we have noted, the police also have their own stereotypes of which are the sections of the public that should be taken notice of. The notion of the 'law-abiding community', as used by Sir Kenneth Newman, can have quite a restrictive effect in a situation in which police have already defined some areas of the city and some social and ethnic groups as 'crime-prone'.

At the present time many of these local liaison committees are in the early stages of developing communication between local councillors, representatives of local community groups and the police. Our argument would be for as wide a participation as possible, to be mobilized by the local councils.

We discuss in Chapter 9 how some of the limitations we have described above might be combated. A recent example illustrates just those limitations. On 21 January 1985 two special police operations began in the Lambeth district of London. A unit of the Special Patrol Group (SPG) was to be used in the Clapham district on uniformed foot patrols with home beat officers, to deter street crime and burglary. Meanwhile the Lambeth district crime squad was to mount an operation, supported by officers experienced in 'targeting and surveillance', to identify and arrest criminals in the Brixton Division. The Lambeth Community–Police Consultative Group in a Press release of 17 January 1985 had announced that it had agreed to the operation with the local police commander, on the understanding that a number of procedures were adhered to, notably that:

(1) The Commander should report back to each meeting of the Group on the way the SPG is being used and its degree of effectiveness . . . (2) The SPG officers should operate as individuals paired with a home beat officer, and not in groups with each other . . . (3) The SPG officers should be briefed on the need to act sensitively, especially in the use of stop and search powers . . . (4) Opportunity must be given for members of the Group to be present at briefings and to go out on patrol with the SPG.

Some of these suggestions are not without merit, particularly the idea that civilian observers should accompany police officers. Others are ill thought out and can only act as a spurious legitimation for 'hard policing', the effects of which are well known. What a 'sensitive use of stop and search powers' involves is anyone's guess. But who did these stipulations come from in the first place?

The elected representatives of the local borough council had a very different view of the matter. In a press release issued on the same day as that of the consultative group, Councillor Gordon Ley, the chairperson of the Borough Police Committee (which in London, of course, has no statutory authority for any aspect of policing) stated:

I am greatly concerned and disturbed by the fact that the police have decided to mount what can only be described as a provocative and disruptive operation in a community where sensitive policing is vital . . . I would like to know if anyone in Brixton has asked for this operation to take place and how the police propose to respond to the anger that it is likely to provoke. 'Swamp 81' is still in most people's memories, and its effects reinforce the need for sensitive policing . . .

In the event, there does not appear to have been anything like the anger that followed on the heels of Swamp 81. But that is not the issue. If Mr Ley and his fellow councillors lose touch with the feelings of the people of Lambeth, then they can be voted out of office. As it was, the statement of a small group of individuals constituting a 'consultative group' flatly contradicted the opinions of the local council and gave the police operation a spurious legitimacy. The issue is not whether the council or the consultative group were correct in their assessments of the operation. It is whether or not a small group of individuals should be presented, in opposition to local elected representatives, as speaking for the public on such a vital act of public policy as a police operation in an area like Brixton.

However, faced with these liaison groups and the need to develop some sort of relationship with them, the Met, it seems, is busy undermining them from within. In November 1984 Sir Kenneth Newman announced his long-awaited plans for the reorganization of the Met, to reduce the size of Scotland Yard's bureaucracy and to give more operational autonomy to the areas. A 'greater freedom of local decision-making' might be welcomed by consultative groups, if it were not that, under the new reorganization, decision-making is to be concentrated in eight new areas. Each area, with the exception of Westminster, will stretch from inner London to outer suburbia, providing the deputy assistant commissioner in charge of each area with a 'mix' of policing problems and a population of about the size that a provincial police force has to control. The 25 Metropolitan Police districts will be abolished and their powers devolved either downwards to the smaller divisions or upwards to the areas. It is this that has thrown the spanner in the works as far as local consultation committees are concerned. As a GLC report spelled out:

> While the present structure is not perfect (only ten boroughs have boundaries coterminous with their police districts), at least up till now there has been some acceptance that the local district commander is responsible for the policing of the borough, and is permitted to discuss his policy with local authority representatives and with the public . . . With reorganization it will take years for the police themselves, let alone the public, to work out where exactly the demarcation of power and responsibility will lie between Scotland Yard, area and division, and thus where demands should be made or with whom discussions initiated. Lambeth, for example, instead of dealing with one commander, will have to relate to four divisional chief superintendents and various area personnel according to the issue under discussion. (GLC 1985, p. 5)

This chapter concludes our survey of what might be called the 'soft' measures which have developed in policing policy in recent years. Apart from some internal problems, a crucial source of contradiction and conflict, which we noted, is their coexistence with the strengthening of the traditional methods of 'hard' policing. To some of these developments we now turn.

7

Technology and Power:
Towards the Police State?

If the 'soft' measures designed to strengthen police relations
with the public and other social service agencies have received
high-profile treatment by the police, other developments have
been given a distinctly lower profile. These are the measures
that pose the greatest direct threat to civil liberties, of which the
development of computerized gathering of 'criminal intelligence', and the new powers included in the Police and Criminal
Evidence Act 1984, are two of the most important. Many
writers have stressed the inherent threat to civil liberties, and
we concur. But what we want to stress here is that such
measures will not achieve the goal they have set themselves –
the effective control of crime. And they will fail because of their
profoundly undemocratic character.

Criminal Intelligence

One of the most controversial responses of the police to the
rise in crime and the relative decrease in information available
to them has been the widespread introduction throughout
British police forces of so-called 'crime intelligence systems'.
Like 'fire brigade' policing, the origins of criminal intelligence
appear to lie in the collapse of unit beat policing in the late
sixties.

Partly because of the controversy surrounding the issue, it

remains a remarkably under-researched aspect of police work. Fairly comprehensive independent studies have been completed of the Lothian and Borders and Thames Valley systems, however (see, for example, Campbell 1979; Baldwin and Kinsey 1982, chapter 3). In addition, an internal Home Office assessment of the Thames Valley Police computer system has recently thrown considerable light on the value of criminal intelligence systems for crime investigation and prevention.

The studies so far suggest that as many as one in ten of the population have open files kept on them by the police. In the Lothian and Borders force, for example, some 80,000 personal files are kept by the CID at police headquarters. It has been reliably estimated that approximately two thirds of the persons named on the files have no criminal record. In addition, a further unknown number of files are kept at each of the divisional and sub-divisional police stations throughout the force area. No provision is made for independent scrutiny of the files or for the weeding of files for inaccurate or outdated information.

The sources of the information contained in criminal intelligence are various: shopkeepers, publicans and taxi drivers are commonly used, as are paid informants and other persons with a vested interest in fostering the good offices of the police. Much of the information is, of necessity, hearsay and gossip. Thus an official job description of an area constable in the Lothian and Borders force, dated March 1981, included the following instructions:

He should

– secure the services of at least one informant in every street, not particularly a paid, professional informant, but someone who knows the inhabitants and is inquisitive enough to find out what is going on;

– get to know where the criminals on his area are living, where they work, with whom they live and associate, vehicles they use, places frequented, whether they spend time away from home, and the occasions they are spending money freely;

– make himself known to local officials, e.g. housing department, social workers, gas and electricity board officials, or anyone who has legitimate access to private houses and premises and is in a position to give information;

– cultivate shopkeepers, tradesmen and garage proprietors who are always a good source of information;

– become familiar with bus drivers and conductors, railway employees, taxi drivers and postmen who are out at varying times throughout the day and night.

Interestingly, very similar phraseology is found in the official description of the functions and duties of 'resident beat constables' in the Merseyside Police Force Orders (May 1983):

To obtain information, it is useful for the area constable to make himself known to local officials, shopkeepers, tradesmen, garage proprietors and other reliable persons who regularly visit or reside in each road or street in the area. He should aim at having a contact who is confident in him in every road and street.

Bus drivers and conductors, railway employees, taxi drivers and postmen are out at varying times throughout the twenty-four hours and can help in many ways. (paras. 43–4)

Just as in the Lothian and Borders Police, police constables in the Merseyside force are instructed that

Information collected should be given to the collator, who will then pass it to the appropriate department and file it for easy reference.

The amount of information passed to the collator by the area constable will indicate his effectiveness. (paras. 46–7)

Most intelligence information is thus collected by uniformed police constables – often, however, working in plain clothes as with the Lothian and Borders 'crime patrols' (see Baldwin and Kinsey 1982) – rather than the CID. The information collected – very often general 'domestic gossip' rather than specifically relating to crimes or offences – is passed daily to a 'collator' (or sometimes the 'divisional' or 'field intelligence officer'), who will generally transfer the details to manual card indexes. Included in the description of the functions and duties of the collator in the Merseyside Police Force Orders are the following instructions:

... duties include the collection and analysis of information of all kinds and the dissemination of this to all interested persons such as contables, supervisory officers, CID officers, Crime Intelligence Bureaux etc.

All items, however insignificant, will be recorded and will be available to all personnel at all times. The collator will decide what information he considers could be of assistance to other intelligence sections, surrounding stations or individual officers, and ensure that such information is passed on.

It should be borne in mind that the Collator's Office should be an Informatin Bureau in addition to a Criminal Intelligence Office and that information of all kinds should be encouraged on the premise that we do know today what we will need tomorrow. (paras. 50, 52, 62)

In addition to the preparation of a daily record sheet and entering and cross-referencing intelligence received in the different vehicle, street, intelligence, *modus operandi* and miscellaneous indices, in Merseyside the collator is also charged with the production of a regular 'bulletin', communicating items of special interest throughout the division. This bulletin, the availability of which is strictly limited for 'security' reasons (para. 66), 'will not contain domestic gossip, lists of disqualified drivers, stolen bicycles, absconders or the complete reiteration of the weekly crime figures'. It should be 'well set out and presented in a manner designed to make it interesting and easily read. Items should be kept to a reasonable minimum' (paras. 65–6).

Specific examples of information held on criminal intelligence systems have not, for good reason, been made readily available (but see Campbell 1979). Recently, however, a cardboard box containing a selection of the Lothian and Borders Police equivalent of the Merseyside collator's bulletin was discovered on a rubbish dump in Edinburgh. Headed 'Criminal Intelligence Information', the 'matters', as they are referred to by the local police, are usually produced twice a week by the divisional intelligence officer and circulated around police stations within the division. The documents found on the rubbish dump had been roughly torn into quarters, and when pieced together not all the sheets were complete, nor were they in a complete series, but nonetheless they provided an interesting sample of seventeen complete and dated sheets of closely printed A4, spanning a period from mid-June to mid-October 1983. (It should be emphasized that relatively little 'domestic gossip' is included in these bulletins, and only 'hard' information deemed to be of interest throughout the division is circulated in this form.)

Each item of information contained in the 'matters' is given an individual reference number. From these it is apparent that some 532 intelligence reports had been circulated in 'C' Division bulletins during the four-month period. Of these over 100 complete entries were recovered from the documents found. They referred to some 175 persons by name, giving in most cases their addresses. The date of birth was provided for 86 persons; 58 were below the age of 25, of whom 34 were 20 or under. The vast majority of references were to males, which accords with earlier findings that the single largest group of people most likely to be subjects of criminal intelligence investigation and surveillance are working-class males below the age of 25.

The documents provide information on 43 persons who had been 'checked out' or 'turned over'. In only one instance was an arrest made: a 20-year-old male who was discovered to be wanted on warrant from the sheriff-court for non-payment of a fine. It is notable that the arrest did not relate to suspicious behaviour or actions at the time of the stop. Two persons were discovered 'in possession': one was a 14-year-old boy who was found in possession of tobacco and cigarette papers 'stolen from the Pakistani shop where he had been working all day', and the other was a 17-year-old male found in possession of syringes. The 'item', in this instance provided by two detective constables, reads as follows:

Seen loitering outside Fraser's in the West End at 4.20 pm, 4 July 1983. He was turned over and found to be in possession of syringes. He was joined by a girl who gave the name Jane Jones who admitted pre-cons for shoplifting (possibly JEAN JONES or BROWN, born 2 September 1963). She was obviously in Fraser's to shoplift but was put off by police presence. Description: dark hair with vivid pink streaks.

Stop-checks such as these are carried out primarily as a means of gathering intelligence both about the people checked and about their associates. Thus one entry refers to a 32-year-old woman being stopped and searched for drugs. No drugs were found but 'she was also [sic] in possession of a list of phone numbers which relate to the following . . .' Five names and addresses are then given with no explanation or reference to criminal records or activity.

Some of the information reported is very basic; one item, for example, refers simply to the change of address of a 16-year-old female who 'is now residing with her parents at . . . She is about three months pregnant.' Another refers cryptically to a 23-year-old man as 'checked out at 12.20 pm, 21 September 1983, in Morrison Street. He was wearing black trousers.' (It may be worth bearing in mind that as in Merseyside, so in Lothian and Borders, an officer's effectiveness is judged by the amount of criminal intelligence he collects.)

Another entry, which caused some local controversy, referred to a man 'seen in the Crosswinds Cafe, Tollcoss, at 5.30 pm 11th inst., accompanied by an unknown female'. The Crosswinds is run by community and voluntary workers as a drop-in centre for the young and unemployed.

There is some evidence of people being repeatedly stopped by reason of their previous conduct rather than their actions at the time. Thus one item refers to two 16-year-old youths on leave from a List D school:

Both are on leave from Wellington Farm and have been seen on numerous occasions in the town section. Both have pre-cons for theft, house-breaking etc., and should be checked out at every opportunity.

Criticisms of the collection of criminal intelligence by the police have in the main focused on the danger of relying on uncorroborated and inaccurate gossip, and on the possibility that bias in the information will lead the police to concentrate resources differentially on certain groups who, for whatever reason, are labelled potential criminals. It has also been pointed out that the kind of non-specific information collected bears little if any relevance to the actual detection of particular offences. Against those who have argued that such methods are offensive to liberty and privacy, those who defend the system maintain that the end justifies the means. Methods and technology which improve the efficiency of the police, and therefore make the streets safer for the 'law-abiding' citizen, justify any minor intrusions into everyday life.

The practical justification of criminal intelligence, namely, that it is a substantial aid to the police in detecting and thereby preventing crime, surely no longer holds water. The findings of an unpublished report of the Scientific Research and Development Branch of the Home Office, reported in the *New Statesman* (29 June 1984), solidly confirm earlier and more speculative criticism (see Baldwin and Kinsey 1982). As part of a study, over three years and six months, of the computerized system of criminal intelligence employed by the Thames Valley Police since 1978, the Home Office researchers sought details of successful uses of the system in the detection of crime. It was established that in 1980 information was requested from the computer indexes – of persons, vehicles, places, occurrences and crimes – on more than 3,000 occasions every week. In terms of crime detection the success rate is staggeringly low. The report merits extended quotation:

(a)   Collators were asked to report details of every instance of a retrieval which had promoted a detection by providing a list of suspects. The returns depended on officers acknowledging that the system was of use and reporting the fact to the collators. During 1980 there were 20 such reports covering the following offences:

Offence	Frequency
Burglary	6
Indecency	6
Theft	2
Traffic offence	2
Obtaining by deception	1
Armed robbery	1
Wounding	1
Nuisance	1

Since some successes will probably have gone unreported, this figure gives a lower limit to the annual success rate.

(b)   The survey, in which officers were asked for details of any 'successes' they themselves had had, indicates that for the force as a whole the annual success rate was about 400. This figure is likely to be an over-estimate (some of the quoted instances of success seemed not to be valid), but it serves as an upper estimate for the number of successes.

On the basis of these data, it can be estimated that in 1980 the number of successes arising from lists of suspects was between 20 and 400, i.e. between 0.03 per cent and 0.6 per cent of the recorded crime. (para. 3.18)

Clearly, even this tiny 'success' rate needs to be tempered by the fact that all that the intelligence system provided was a list of suspects, each one of whom would need specific investigation, so that at best crime intelligence only acts as an aid to detection in a tiny proportion of investigations. The report concludes that it is 'impossible to detect any change in the crime statistics that can be unambiguously attributed to the presence of this system' (para. 2.1). Even so, it may be said that the use of crime intelligence is valid if only one criminal is brought to book. However, if we look at the manpower tied up in such systems – and therefore taken off more orthodox methods of crime investigation such as interviewing witnesses – there is surely room to question any such claim. The Thames Valley system entails the use of 32 police constables, two sergeants, one inspector and 11 clerical assistants. Thirty-five police officers are thus deployed full-time in office duties at considerable cost in salaries and minimal effect in crime detection.

While the impact on crime detection thus appears to be at best marginal, many commentators have expressed concern that the impact at street level will nonetheless be intense. In analysing the intelligence items included in the Lothian and Borders bulletins, the large number of stop-checks was noted and it was suggested that the tactic had been employed as a routine method of collecting such information. There must be some considerable ground for concern that as these practices grow, so the very problem they have been set up to deal with – namely, the lack of information provided voluntarily by the public – will, as with 'fire brigade' policing, only be compounded and the police driven further along the cul-de-sac they have already entered. But again, we would see these developments indicating primarily a lack of foresight rather than an evil plot. However, when combined with the introduction of the new police powers of stop and search, identification, detention and interrogation introduced in recent legislation, we must not only question such innovations in terms of the efficient investigation and control of crime, but we must also look to broader social and political consequences of such a radical departure from the principles of democratic policing.

The wide-spread practice of intelligence collection in many ways justifies the fears expressed in relation to police-initiated Neighbourhood Watch schemes. To our certain knowledge, in one force area the contact officers for Neighbourhood Watch are in fact the sub-divisional collators, and the schemes are regarded as a valuable source of information. As we have been at pains to emphasize, this does not devalue the project of Neighbourhood Watch, *provided* the political and organizational structure of the police force concerned is open, democratic and accountable. We would even go so far as to say that in specific circumstances efficient crime investigation and detection will warrant the use of covert surveillance and intelligence collection: serious drugs cases might be a case in point. However, especially in the light of large-scale investigations such as the Yorkshire Ripper inquiry, we doubt the efficacy of large-scale data banks, even in relation to serious crimes; and where such information is collected, it should be closely monitored by police authorities empowered to inspect data – that is, by local government. Under no circumstances – for reasons both of civil liberties and of cost-effectiveness – should the use of such systems be anything but exceptional. Again, it needs to be said that the acceptability of the particular practice is dependent absolutely on the political structure and accountability of the police.

The Police and Criminal Evidence Act 1984

Criticism of the Police and Criminal Evidence Act (PACE) has concentrated quite correctly on the erosion of civil liberties, on the vagueness of its wording, and on the possibility of wide-ranging interpretation by both commissioners and police officers on the beat. Some writers on the left are concerned to see PACE as symptomatic of the police 'concerning them-selves less with crime detection and more with social control and public order. Their new position and role mirrors the new philosophy of policing in the new Police [Act]. It is a philosophy of coercion and not of consent' (Christian 1983, p. 210).

While it is without doubt the case that the provisions of PACE will be used against political organizations, so have the provisions of much older legislation. It is a mistake to see the use of the police in a coercive political role as something that emerges for the first time with PACE. As Baldwin and Kinsey have shown (1982, chapter 7), one of the most significant antecedents of PACE was police pressure on the Royal Commission on Criminal Procedure (1981) to recommend the legalization of many existing police practices with regard to such matters as the interrogation of suspects. There is no evidence to suggest that the police at that time were thinking of political suspects rather than those involved in burglary or theft. The point we wish to make about PACE is not only that its provisions constitute a threat to civil liberties, but that it is counterproductive from the standpoint of the major police task it is intended to assist – the control of crime. It is counter-productive because it strengthens those very aspects of polic-ing, such as stop and search, which alienate those sections of the community with information about crime.

Part 1 of PACE codifies and extends existing powers of stop and search, empowering 'any constable acting on reasonable grounds for suspicion, to stop, detain, and search, persons or vehicles, or anything in or on a vehicle, for certain items which may be seized' (*Law Society Gazette*, 3 April 1985). The PSI report on the Metropolitan Police concluded:

Our findings show that the stops made in London (amounting to well over a million a year) result in the detection of a very substantial number of offences – perhaps more than 100,000 a year. Even if the police are exceeding their formal powers it is difficult to argue that a method that leads to the detection of so many offences should be abandoned. On the other hand, since most people who are stopped are innocent, it is clear that current practice runs the serious risk of 'causing offence to innocent persons'. (PSI 1983, vol. 1, p. 311)

The survey found that 11 per cent of stops produced a 'result' (p. 116). Now such a rate is surprisingly high: a one in ten arrest rate would seem, at first sight, to indicate that the police were acting with remarkable prescience in who they stopped to search. However, in terms of the efficacy of crime control this is a mistaken view – for two reasons.

Take first the nature of the offences for which the 11 per cent were arrested. If these had been burglary, or carrying firearms, or having committed sexual assaults, one might readily concede the necessity of stop and search for an effective police force protecting the community, including the 90 per cent of innocents who get caught in stop and search. But this is not the case. The people involved were arrested for a motley of petty offences. This conclusion is borne out in our Merseyside surveys, from which it appears that only 43 arrests are made per 1,000 stops. Of these arrests, 8 are for theft, 5 are for drunken driving, 5 for burglary and 3 for unauthorized taking of a motor vehicle. Possession of drugs and of offensive weapons each account for 3 arrests per 1,000 stops. The remainder are made up of arrests for drunkenness, disorderly behaviour, criminal damage, etc.

The low productivity in stop and search operations as regards serious crime has to be balanced against the alienating effect on the vast majority of innocents stopped. Again the PSI report gives evidence of this in the form of a direct relationship between adverse opinion of the police and the frequency of being stopped. Thus 60 per cent of people who had been stopped by the police three or more times in the previous year believed that the police stopped people (on foot) without sufficient reason, compared to 15 per cent of people who had never been stopped. Likewise, 44 per cent of people stopped three or more times felt that ethnic minorities were not treated fairly by the police, compared with 17 per cent of those who had never been stopped (PSI 1983, vol. 1, chapter 4).

On the face of it, then, the most important consequence of stop and search is the alienation of the public from the police rather than the apprehension of a significant number of serious offenders. Yet it is the strengthening of stop and search powers that was one of the major aims of PACE. Defenders of the 1984 Act and of stop and search as a necessary element in policing strategy may point to recent innovations, some of them included in PACE itself, which, it could be argued, are designed to counter the negative effects of stop and search. There are four such arguments which are worth considering.

The recording of stops. Included in the provisions of PACE is the requirement that police officers conducting stop and search state their name, the object of the search, and the grounds for making it. There is a statutory right for a person searched to obtain a record of the search 'within a year'. However, the Act also states that the police have to record a search 'unless it is not practicable to do so'. Baldwin and Kinsey (1985) point out that PACE in this respect shifts the accountability of police behaviour significantly away from being subject to the review of the courts towards internal police discretion:

> The opportunity for officers to sidestep these provisions is built into the legislation itself. The Act demands not that any search should be recorded but only 'a search in excercise of any such power' (under the Police and Criminal Evidence Act, section 1). Thus the recording procedure is always avoided when a person allows a search voluntarily – knowing perhaps that if he or she dissents, more rigorous formal powers will be used. If a searched person asks for a copy of a search record and this is refused because 'you allowed the search voluntarily' or because 'it was not practicable to record the search – we were too busy' there may be little comeback. (p. 95)

It is in any case difficult to imagine how the annoyance and indignity of stop and search, especially among those sections of the community, such as young blacks, who are already aware that they are the objects of police prejudice and discrimination, could be mitigated by the formal right to a piece of paper stating the object of the exercise.

The Metropolitan Police code of ethics. In April 1985 the Met was issued with a document entitled 'The Principles of Policing and Guidance for Professional Behaviour'. This code, initiated by Sir Kenneth Newman, enjoins police officers to adhere to numerous principles of good behaviour, among which are:

To uphold the rule of law by sustaining wholeheartedly . . . the presumption of innocence: and by scrupulous compliance with the requirements of reasonableness when acting upon suspicion, the rules pertaining to the rights of suspects; the restrictions upon powers of arrest and detention, and the requirement for integrity in the collection and presentation of evidence.

To show compassionate respect for the dignity of the individual and to treat every person of whatever social position, race or creed with courtesy and understanding.

Any code of ethics that could really enforce the criterion of 'reasonable suspicion' as a principle governing police officers' conduct might be expected to have a profound effect in reducing the large number of arbitrary stops. Again, as the PSI study points out:

In a substantial proportion of cases where stops were reported in the survey of police officers, the officer did not give what we judge to be a 'good' reason for making the stop. We could see no good reason for the stop in one third of the cases recorded in the course of our observational work, and, closely in accord with this, the survey of Londoners shows that for 38 per cent of stops the person involved thinks the police had no good reason for making the stop. (PSI 1983, vol. 4, p. 321)

But the enforcement of such a principle, in a police force whose occupational culture is characterized by such a high degree of racist and sexist prejudice, combined with a maximum of autonomy for officers on patrol, is beset with difficulties. The circumstances under which such a code of behaviour might be enforced are precisely those, which we specify in the next chapter, of increased public scrutiny of the police and the accountability of police policy and behaviour to a wider public.

Community liaison. The Scarman Report regarded community liaison committees (mentioned in Chapter 6) as a crucial mechanism whereby the police could explain to the public the 'occasional necessity' for stop and search operations of the Swamp 81 variety. Indeed, it was largely because of Scarman's conclusion that the statutory requirement for such committees was included in PACE. We have already commented on the undemocratic nature of such bodies and shown how they can easily become mechanisms for giving police operations a spurious legitimacy, rather than securing the agreement of the local community. Of course, it is quite possible to envisage circumstances in which a major stop and search operation *would* be necessary. But the conditions under which the public would concede the necessity for it, particularly if it impinged on their personal liberty, would be that it should accord with the criteria for the mounting of such operations set down by a democratically elected police authority.

Targeting. Following the inner-city riots of 1981 and the widespread public criticism of stop and search, 'targeting' – the observation and tracking of particular known offenders – was being presented as a more sophisticated alternative. On a tour of London's police stations in October 1982, Sir Kenneth Newman claimed that street robbers would soon be pursued in 'a much more professional way'. According to a *Guardian* report (14 October 1982), 'Targeting is Sir Kenneth's alternative to the largely discredited "swamping" approach of trying to contain street crime by large-scale stop and search operations. Swamp 81 in Brixton played a part in the build-up of last year's riots. But Sir Kenneth, giving a press conference during his tour of London police stations, did not rule out 'big operations'. Nor, of course, was there any intention of doing so. The provisions of PACE would have made little sense if stop and search was being phased out as a major element in the police strategy. It should be clear that any talk of targeting replacing stop and search is largely a public relations exercise. If the vast bulk of street crime is opportunist and performed by young people drifting in and out of crime, the methods of tracking and surveillance of known offenders make little sense. Or, perhaps, such methods become a polite term for criminal intelligence-gathering operations directed at large sections of the community and having the same alienating effect on public attitudes to the police as stop and search itself.

Towards a Police State?

Both the development of criminal intelligence and the strengthening of 'hard' policing powers by PACE will, we have suggested, make little contribution to the fight against crime. This does not imply, however, that their real purpose lies elsewhere. The criticism of current policing strategies is not that their *real* task is the control of political protest, with crime as a mere footnote to their concerns. Rather, it is that as the arm of a highly bureaucratized and undemocratic state machine, they are only capable of responding to real social problems in ways which reflect that bureaucratic character – and consequently cannot succeed. Undemocratic, unaccountable state organs are grossly inefficient, even when they try to tackle genuine social problems, among which crime is to be included.

This having been said, though, it is important to remember that Britain is a class-divided society. It is also a deeply racist and sexist society. It is committed to a suicidal policy of nuclear defence. It is in the midst of a grave economic crisis. In such circumstances the escalation of social protest is inevitable. What is equally inevitable is that ruling elites with a vested interest in the status quo will attempt to present much of that protest as a form of criminality and 'a threat to law and order'. It is worthwhile reminding ourselves that the criminalization of social protest is of advantage to ruling elites precisely because of the public's antipathy to the real social problem of crime. If social protest can be associated in the public mind with crime, then its disapproval in the eyes of the public is secured. It is therefore precisely *because* the police fulfil such a vital service to the public (though with gross inefficiency and with harmful side effects) that placing the control of political protest in their hands is such an attractive policy for powerful groups in society opposed to change and reform.

It is in this light that the proposal in the 1985 Public Order Bill to give the police new powers to control public demonstrations, must be viewed.

Addendum: The Riots of Autumn 1985 and the Legacy of Scarman

In this and the preceding chapters we have argued that 'hard' policing – computer surveillance, increased police stop-and-search powers, cannot coexist without underming the 'soft' measures of community relations and multi-agency policing. Furthermore we have argued that 'soft' policing which falls short of full police accountability to local government is not likely to be successful in restoring community confidence in the police. These fears were graphically confirmed in the autumn of 1985 (after most of this book had already been written) by the worst series of inner-city riots witnessed in this country in modern times.

The events in Handsworth, Brixton, Toxteth, and Tottenham confirmed not only our analysis but the collective political amnesia of politicians.

The familiar argument between the Tory right wing and much of the Labour Party that was conducted after the riots of 1981 has been repeated with no increase in sophistication. From the Tory Right there was Douglas Hurd's marvellous juxtaposition that the riot in Handsworth was 'crime' and 'not a social phenomenon' and Norman Tebbit's announcement during the Tory Party conference that the riots were an outbreak of human wickedness. From the Labour Party Gerald Kaufman argued that the riots showed that the recommendations of the Scarman report of 1981 had been ignored or swept under the carpet, and called for a further

judicial inquiry into the causes. The question that no commentators have apparently asked is to what extent, four years
on, the new outbreak of rioting revealed contradictions in
the original Scarman recommendations. Scarman had both
strengths and weaknesses. He was able, like many liberal
commentators, to see urban decay and deprivation compounded
by racism and oppressive policing as the main causes of the
1981 riots. A much weaker element, and not the central focus
of his analysis, was the political marginalization of the poor,
their lack of effective participation in controlling the decisions
that affect them. It is not poverty *per se* that causes riots, but
the feeling of frustration that comes from comparing oneself to
surrounding affluent communities while feeling convinced
that there are no effective channels through which one's
grievances can be dealt with. Scarman showed awareness of
this only in an aside towards the end of his report: 'local
communities should be more fully involved in the decisions
which affect them . . . Local communities must be fully and
effectively involved in planning, in the provision of local
services, and in the management and financing of specific
projects' (Scarman 1981, p. 101).

Such a call for 'involvement' was weakened, ambiguous and
has been largely forgotten. It is clear that local control over
the distribution of job opportunities and investment funds is
diminishing (with the abolition of West Midlands Metropolitan
Council in 1986 will go the West Midlands Enterprise Board,
which is concerned with arresting the economic decline of the
area).

As for Scarman's failure to call for police accountability
(rather than community policing and community consultation
forums), events in Handsworth clearly illustrate that the issue
will not go away. It appears that with the appointment of
Geoffrey Dear as Chief Constable of the West Midlands, the
community policing strategy in the area pioneered in the late
1970s by David Webb was replaced by a 'get tough' approach,
particularly regarding drug dealers.

A number of commentators and locals were reported as

arguing that the buying and selling of cannabis is the sole form of livelihood for a large section of the Handsworth young black community and therefore any attempt to stop it was going to be economically disastrous for a large number of youths: riot was inevitable under such circumstances. Thus the *Guardian* on 11 October 1985 quoted a local black:

Us guys we just sell weed, nothing heroin . . . Most of us have three, four, five kids, we got no jobs, all we can do is sell the weed. If we can't hustle there's nothing for us and nothing for the kids. If we can't sell our weed then we is going to do armed robbery. If they don't leave us alone we're going to burn them down, that's fucking truth.

The drugs problem was reiterated by Geoffrey Dear when speaking to the West Midlands Police Committee, but he added a new and alarming dimension. According to *The Times* of 16 October 1985:

Mr Dear agreed that a blind eye might have been turned by the police in the past to small cannabis dealings in the area and that a change in policy towards drug dealing could have been responsible for the trouble. Main dealers in heroin and cocaine were finding their livelihood threatened by the enlarged West Midlands drug squad.

He was quoted directly as saying 'I believe it is these people who were behind this riot, acting in defence of enormous profits. We have an influx of heroin and cocaine coming into Birmingham at the moment.' The argument is that an agreement with a section of the local community to ignore certain offences in return for cooperation had to be abandoned by the police as the drugs situation in Birmingham changed. In fact, it seems, the 'blind eye' policy extended to more than soft drugs: a local black trader told the *Guardian* that Handsworth was a 'no go area' or a free city as far as certain offences were concerned. 'He said that previously offences like having no tax disc on a car or the possession and sale of cannabis had not been prosecuted in Handsworth under a "tacit agreement" between the community and the police' (*Guardian* 11 October 1985).

Geoffrey Dear was apparently arguing that as more hard drugs were coming into the area the 'no go' policy on drugs offences in general had had to be abandoned. But an additional element in precipitating the riot appears to have been the pressure from residents for the police to get tough on drugs dealing in general. Local residents approached the police to stop a bingo hall being turned into an amusement arcade which, it was felt, would increase drugs-related activity in the area. So the police, now under pressure from a different section of the community, either felt pressured, or used the occasion to change previous policy on drugs and hence create riot conditions. It can be argued that a police-initiated 'no go' policy regarding certain types of offences will help police community relations as long as there is a community consensus that the offences concerned are trivial. Such a strategy of community policing in this case had laid down problems for the future. The police, having allowed the ganja economy to develop in the area by easing off on action against dealers, were now facing increasing pressure from residents in the area to take a harder line on drug pushers. Both white and black residents were no doubt concerned about the appearance of hard drugs alongside cannabis. The whole assumption behind the argument that a 'go softly' policy on ganja had to end because of the increasing threat of heroin and cocaine coming into the area is that the taking and selling of hard drugs are inextricably linked.

It might appear to be particularly necessary for the police not to be too tightly constrained by consultation procedures where drugs are concerned. Such was Scarman's intent. 'Neither', he had warned, 'will consultation always produce an agreed result: in the end it will be necessary for the appropriate police commander to take a decision' (Scarman 1981, p. 92). The *Guardian* spoke on 11 October 1985 of the 'fine and desperately difficult line' between rightly pursuing drug dealers while trying to avoid the harassment of 'youths smoking the odd joint'. But the line is quite clear and, importantly, it is widely recognized by the public. Survey after survey has revealed a virtual consensus over the type of crime against which the public want the police to act. Burglary, sexual attacks on women, assault and heroin are the priorities. Cannabis is not: indeed it is usually rated as something the police should spend less time on. Police priorities are not in line with the interests of the people. This is one reason why there is a lack of public cooperation. With such help the police would have much better information, from cannabis smokers among others, about where the dangerous drugs like heroin were being peddled. The idea that in adjusting policing to community needs the police inevitably come across a conflict of standards and cultures of the different ethnic communities regarding the use of hard drugs is nonsense. There is no community out there – apart from some junkies – who actually condone such activity. To argue otherwise is a racist slur on the black community.

Of course the police 'know' that heroin is coming into the West Midlands in increasing quantities, but they do not know where it actually is or who is selling it because they have little real contact with the people on the streets. The sudden police action shattered the 'calm' of community policing, with pathetic results. A pub in Handsworth was raided and the result was a modest amount of ganja. Where were the quantities of hard drugs and the 'seven drug barons' which the West Midlands Drug Squad claimed to be after? The only tangible result was the riot itself, an outbreak of violence which further divided the community, increased the alienation of youth and destroyed many of the scant facilities which the community had.

Scarman thus advocated and made respectable a type of police–community consultation in which the police are free to take notice of one section of the community at one time and another, or none, the next – with no guarantee that police priorities will necessarily reflect those of the community. He advocated, furthermore, that community policing could coexist with 'hard policing' – the type of 'hard policing' involving stop and search – and the type of surveillance which alienates precisely those sections of young people in the inner cities who have most information about crime. One of the consequences of this, as we have argued, is that attempts to bring the police closer to the community and hence increase the flow of information is undermined by 'hard' policing.

One indication of this in Handsworth comes from a study of one of the main initiatives in community policing in the area, the 'Lozells Project'. Set up in 1979, the project involved 'multi-agency' cooperation between police, education social services and probation workers. Among the main activities of the project were police-sponsored youth clubs and close contact between police and schools. Guy Cumbernatch was sent by the Home Office to monitor the effects of the project. In an article published in *New Society* on 2 October 1985, shortly after the riots, he reported that 'in terms of its real aims it was a manifest failure. We found that it seemed to achieve little in the way of more positive attitudes to the police.' Looking at the effect of police lecturers visiting local schools to talk about police work, Cumbernatch and his team found that 'children expected "school officers" to be better than "police in general" (more educated, friendly and so on). . . . .after the course, the children thought that the police officers were less intelligent, less educated, and less friendly than they had expected. Given that children did not expect to be exposed to typical police officers, it is hardly surprising that attitudes to "police in general" did not change.'

Cumbernatch came up with similar findings in the police-run youth clubs of the Lozells Project. This is clear evidence of the working through of some of the inner contradictions of Scarman. The powerful argument for local democratic account-ability is that a community which trusts the police because they are answerable to them will provide the type of information flow about serious crime which will make 'hard' policing totally unnecessary.

The issue of policing is linked to the other social issues facing the inner city, then, not simply because crime and police matters are every bit as real a manifestation of decay as homelessness and unemployment. The issue of local demo-cratic accountability of the police relates to the issue of local participation in the control of other state agencies as a way of overcoming the increasing marginaliztion of the inner-city populations out of participation in the political system. This marginalization lies behind the effective re-emergence of riot in its eighteenth-century guise – a form of political expression for those marginalized from all other modes of articulating their interests and making their voices heard. On this matter there was, in some quarters, a deal more sophistication than in 1981. A *Guardian* editorial said on 12 September:

There is, though no politician of any major party cares to admit it, a link between the stabbings and stampedes on football's terraces and the bubbling mayhem of our inner cities. White or black, unemployed or fitfully employed, the rioters belong to the desolate deprived underclass of modern Britain's urban ghettos. They are not in any real sense part of the communities whose 'community leaders' bestride our television screens (ask yourself truthfully if you live in an inner city: what is your community? Who is your leader?) They do not vote or join trades unions or write to the local MP. They are beyond the reach of conventionally organised politics. Their family life is a fractured nullity. Their homes are run down hovels. Education has passed them by. They have no marketable skills. They are without immediate hope or immediate purpose in society.

As we have said before, local democratic police accountability is part of a process of solving a fundamental problem: the real time bomb ticking away in our inner cities is the combination of relative deprivation and political marginalization con-sequent upon economic marginalization. We have to devise new forms of political integration which do not any longer depend on having a stable job. This means popular participation in setting policing priorities, in deciding how urban pro-gramme funds are going to be used, in deciding how local investment plans are going to be constructed. The fight for police accountability is all of a piece with the fight against the dismantlement of local government and for greater decentralization of power and decision-making. To answer those who say this will only lead to more bickering and clashes of interest within local communities, we argue that however difficult it will be in the short run, it is vital if communities are to be constructed and preserved in the face of the most massive economic and social transformation this country has seen since the industrial revolution.

8

Discretion and Accountability: Proposals for a New Police Authority

We have looked at the crisis in policing and at the measures which the police have taken in response to that crisis. We have argued that they are contradictory, ineffective, and in some cases a threat to civil liberties. In this and the following chapter we shall attempt to portray an alternative view: one which links the capacity of the police to provide a service that the community want with the democratic accountability of the police to the community. Democracy and effectiveness are inextricably linked.

It follows that any change in the role of the police and an increase in their efficiency must involve a fundamental transformation both of the institutions surrounding the police and of the internal structure of policing. The Conservative contention that a massive increase in resources and the granting to the police of virtual freedom of action will achieve a crime-free Britain is false. In fact, the very opposite would occur – indeed, it is already happening. The alternative, liberal, notion, that the reform of, and greater reliance on, the rule of law will do the trick, is optimistic in the extreme. It fundamentally underestimates the problems involved: namely, that police discretion is inevitable, and that the structural biases inherent in police organization inevitably predispose police officers to exercise discretion in particular ways and in particular directions.

Police work routinely involves choices: whether to institute proceedings; whether to ignore or focus upon specific offences, suspects, or populations; whether to invoke formal rules or procedures or to resolve the matter informally without reference to the criminal justice system. Much of the current political controversy over the accountability of the police is reducible to the root questions of the limited efficacy of rules and the extent of discretion. Conventionally there are three approaches to these matters, which are embodied in three distinct conceptions of policing.

The Liberal–Constitutionalist Model of Policing

This is the classic model which assumes the independence of the police within the orthodox conception of the separation of powers and the supremacy of Parliament. Not surprisingly, it is the model selectively favoured by chief constables, as with one fell swoop it asserts their political neutrality and relieves them of responsibility for the actions of their officers.

The police, so the argument goes, merely enforce the law. They do not make policy or engage in political decision-making, and therefore should not be subject to 'party political' pressure (that is, accountability), whether through central or local government. Whatever their rank, police officers, it is claimed, are individually responsible for their actions and subject to the ordinary law of the land and to the courts, just like any other member of the public. The police officer is but a citizen in uniform. Responsibility for policing is thus treated as a matter of law rather than of politics, to be dealt with individually, not collectively.

This model dismisses the *de facto* policy-making and political role of the police, just as it ignores the increased institutional and legal divide between police and public exemplified in the Police and Criminal Evidence Act 1984. Who, after that legislation, can seriously argue that the liberal–constitutionalist model is an accurate reflection of the nature of policing?

Nonetheless, there is one aspect of the model which stands in its favour: the *belief* that the powers exercised by a police officer should, in principle, be no different from those available to the ordinary member of the public.

The Market Model and the New Right

This model lays claim to a radical *laisser-faire* philosophy in which the police respond or react solely upon public complaint or demand: 'The reactive mobilization system portrays an *entrepreneurial model of the law*. It assumes that citizens will voluntarily and rationally pursue their own interests, with the greatest good of the greatest numbers presumptively arising from the selfish enterprise of the atomised mass. It is the legal analogue of the market economy' (Black 1980, p. 52). Under this system of policing, individual members of the public are left to evaluate the seriousness of an incident in terms of individual injury, annoyance, damage to property and so on; the seriousness of the incident is assumed to be reflected in the decision to report it to the police. There are a number of limitations to this approach.

First, it is wrong to assume that because a crime is not reported it is not serious, nor can the *social* costs of vandalism, for example, be calculated solely in terms of financial or other damage to individuals. Second, even without taking into account the level of unreported crime, demand will frequently exceed supply. Furthermore, as far as policing is concerned, the supply of resources is inelastic. Supply cannot adjust itself to demand and depends absolutely on policy criteria.

It is the idea of the market model that underlies the simple Tory rhetoric of 'more officers, more powers and more technology' as the response to crime. The problem is that it is neither financially possible nor politically desirable to keep on increasing police powers and resources in this way. It will always be necessary for someone other than the victim of a crime to select priorities, take policy decisions and ration resources according to non-market criteria. The market model ignores the fundamental need for overall policy-making, public debate and collective democratic control. It also ignores the manner in which police institutional interests and police occupational culture may override public demand. However, to the limited extent that the police do comply with public demand, there is some truth in the claim that this model of policing has a radically democratic character.

The Left–Idealist Model

In this model the police at present are seen as a monolithic and contradiction-free manifestation of state power. They are presented as the strong right arm of the state, and exercise an exclusively political function directed towards the criminalization and repression of working-class political activity. Unlike the market model, public demand is denigrated: far from being a rational expression of self-interest, the need for police action felt by working-class people is merely a construction of media–police manipulation. Fear of crime is portrayed as an irrational response engendered by moral panic.

In stark contrast to both the liberal–constitutionalist and the market models, the left–idealist demands outright political control of policing in all its dimensions, that is to say, full operational control of the police by elected police authorities. This can only be achieved after a radical recomposition of state power. In the meantime a policy of opposition and 'negative accountability' is followed – that is, the monitoring of police behaviour and the exposing of repressive and illegal police activity. Any notion of the reform of policing practices or any concern with crime as a social problem is met with a nihilistic scepticism.

Nevertheless, there is some value in this model and it lies in the emphasis given to the need for political accountability and the recognition of the inherently political and coercive nature of policing. As we shall see, there is a need for an interventionist role on the part of government, particularly local government. However, the demand for total operational control is self-evidently impracticable, even in an idealized post-revolutionary world. In the meantime, the concept of 'negative account-ability' denies the possibility, or present value, of public participation in any form of dialogue or communication with the police, as exemplified in the GLC's and some London Labour boroughs' refusal to participate in consultative panels.

The Necessity for Discretion

Under the liberal–constitutionalist model the presence of discretion in the system is a sign of fault in the design. The law should and can provide the right answer to all problems of crime. It can be woven into the seamless web which covers all exigencies. Such failures in design that do occur, lead to arbitrary justice in which the neutrality of the law is impeached. Similarly, police officers, like judges, never make the law – they merely implement it to the best of their ability. Failure of the rule of law wherever it occurs is a product of badly trained police officers and laws which have been ill conceived and faultily drafted. This results in privilege and advantage for some, disadvantage and discrimination for others; it engenders disenchantment, and brings the law and its institutions into disrepute. Increased professionalism and a tighter legality reduce the scope of discretion and its necessity, and, by the same token, increase public confidence in the police and the efficiency of the criminal justice system. Objectivity, neutrality and responsibility are invoked in the name of police profes-sionalism and guaranteed in the framework of rules of law. To mend and improve the system we must adjust the law and secure its correct application.

For the left–idealist the key to understanding the essence of the law and the true nature of police work lies in the gap between rules and reality. Discretion is not a failure of legality but the locus of real power behind the smokescreen of the rule of law. 'Justice', such as it is, occurs without the limit of the law; it is always substantive justice, but it is partial and particular – the substantive justice of the ruling class. Discretion is systematically exercised by the police against the working class in favour of the powerful. Thus the rhetoric of law and order and the 'fight against crime' are the mask behind which the strong state grows. Even those laws introduced in the interests of the working class are ignored or used against them. The rule-free cinema world of Dirty Harry is, for once, an accurate version of reality.

In the market model, however, discretion ('free choice') is exercised by the individual consumer. The police merely respond within the rules and supply in direct accord with demand. Paradoxically, however, some Conservatives share a belief in the irrelevance of rules, but on the grounds that rules are irrelevant to the preservation of order. In a perplexed society, extraordinary measures are required to hold the social fabric together and to counter the threat of anarchy. This is the job of the police, who must make and maintain order out of the chaos in which law is impossible. History shows this to be so. Over the years the trustworthiness and expertise of the police have been established. To pursue the principle and the letter of the law is to forget the real purpose and let the guilty go free.

Thus the constitutionalists and the left–idealists share a profound distrust of police discretion and, for different reasons, seek to eradicate it. The right, on the other hand, would deny it was a problem. In our view, while the exercise of open-ended discretionary powers is clearly abhorrent (and also unnecessary), there are three essential reasons for recognizing the role of discretion in policing. First, the nature of rules and the ambiguity of language require the interpretation of general rules to fit particular situations – two examples might be the definition of 'reasonable suspicion' and of an 'offensive weapon'. Belief in the closed structure of law is practically and logically impossible. Nonetheless, formal rules are not in any sense redundant; they provide the outer limits to legitimate action. The problem arises at the moment of interpretation. for although interpretation is always necessary, not every interpretation is desirable. For this reason the criminal law must always be informed by policy, and policy must be informed by politics. The exercise of discretion and the enforcement of law are therefore matters of political rather than legal definition. The strict neutrality and impartiality of the police are an impossibility and not even desirable.

Second, the exercise of discretion is inevitable, given the limited resources available in any society. It is impossible to enforce all laws on the statute book or to pursue every person committing a criminal offence. Priorities have to be decided upon. Once again, policing becomes a matter of politics, given that there could never be enough police to deal with all crime. The problem is not how many police, but in what way and for what ends the police are to be used.

Third, discretion is desirable because both justice and effective policing demand it. In terms of justice, formal rules cannot make allowance for individual differences and variations in conditions. For example, the theft of five pounds *from* an old-age pensioner is substantively different from the theft of five pounds *by* a pensioner. Effective police work demands the recognition of substantive differences and the deployment of resources accordingly. Efficient police work demands practical judgement based on past experience and accumulated knowledge. Although decisions on substantive grounds are desirable, it is again a matter for policy and politics to determine. Equality at law does not mean that for every offence every person is equally suspect, but preference or deference on grounds of social status, gender or race must be avoided. Universal suspicion of all sections of the population for every crime would not only be unworkable, it would be politically intolerable. However, it is vital to distinguish between practically based generalizations on the one hand and prejudiced stereotyping on the other. Further, practical policing must take into account local and regional variations at particular times and under particular conditions. Thus as John Alderson has said of Brixton, 'In order to enforce your law, you end up with three or four million pounds worth of property burnt to the ground. You may think you're being efficient in enforcing your laws . . . but look at it, the place is burning around you . . . I mean, do you enforce the Litter Act in the Mile End Road, the same way as you would in Belgravia?' (Baldwin and Kinsey 1982). Self-evidently not, although the difficult relation between national policy and local demands must not be obscured. Again, it is a matter of political determination: to argue against the prosecution of ganja-smoking in Brixton does not mean that demands for racial discrimination in working men's clubs in Leeds are to be met.

Discretion is thus not to be seen as necessarily a failure, nor as inevitably prejudicial to the powerless, nor – precisely because of this – as a matter for the police to determine as they will. Discretion, by definition, cannot be limited by law. By definition, police work is about politics. At the moment, however, the politics of the police are buried within their existing organizational structures, and ideologically denied in the rhetoric of police professionalism. We have argued that a politics of the police is inevitable, and a certain politics desirable. Change demands a recognition of these facts and a radical institutional reorganization which would allow the inevitable to accord with the desirable.

The Relative Autonomy of the Police

The left–idealist and the liberal–constitutionalist model share a hierarchical conception of police command structures. The idealists conceive of the state as a unitary, monolithic structure organized to one end – namely, the protection of ruling-class interests. Police organizations are thus wielded by the powerful, and consequently the drift towards the 'strong state' can be initiated and steered by those in control – the Home Office and the Association of Chief Police Officers. James Anderton

(Chief Constable of Greater Manchester) might be seen, from this standpoint, to represent the true voice of the ruling class, while John Alderson (until recently Chief Constable of Devon and Cornwall) is perceived as mystifying the stark reality of class oppression.

In this view the history of policing is seen as only tangentially related to crime. The control of crime is seen as an excuse by means of which to develop ever more sophisticated techniques of surveillance, manipulation and coercion. The emphasis is placed upon the policing of strikes, demonstrations and public order, while 'mundane crime' is ignored. The political project must thus be to expose the real nature of the police state rather than to address the problem of crime. The major deficiency of this analysis is the overemphasis on the *coherence* of the police as an institution and their interconnection with all other agencies of the state. It ignores both the social basis of conflict *within* the police and the degree of autonomy of the police in relation to other state agencies. In so doing it denies the existence of political space for reform and the possibility of alternative forces of organization and control.

The idealists, then, see police officers as direct agents of their senior officers who, in turn, are servants of the ruling class. And insofar as they relate to the powerful, they are split off from the people. The police are seen to be isolated from the community spatially, socially, in terms of their aspirations to rise from their lower-middle-class origins, and above all, in terms of the actual job they do – the social control of working-class intransigence. In this model police officers are typified as sharing a common ideology and ruling-class values: a disciplined cadre with a clear structure of operational command and control outside of due process.

The constitutionalist sees the situation in a different light: the comparatively humble class origins of the police allow them to have at least a modicum of shared experience with the wider public, and their fight against crime allows them to gain public sympathy and support. What constitutionalists see as necessary is the correct political control and reform in order to get a good job done more efficiently. They recognize that a degree of police discretion and autonomy does exist, but it is abhorrent to them. It is the task of reform to bring the police directly in line with public policy. Here the conception of the police hierarchy is one of total legal rationality and the efficacy of rules. The duties and the powers of the police are stipulated at law and specified in the multiplicity of force orders. The structure of command is legitimated by the authority of law and due process. It is as if the Weberian ideal type of legal rational decision-making has become a reality.

Both positions have a hierarchical conception of decision-making, which in effect denies the real significance and extent of the discretionary power exercised at street level by the individual police officer. Both neglect the existence of conflict within police organizations, and ignore the processes of negotiation and reconstruction between reality and rules. Both envisage an actual or possible direct connection between those at the top of the hierarchy and those at the bottom. The conception of a force effectively and mechanistically controlled from the centre is relevant to the strategically planned policing operations such as were criticized during the miners' strike of 1984–5. However, it hardly applies to routine policing where issues are diverse, resources widely spread, and supervision minimal.

The market model clearly rejects any such hierarchical conception of law enforcement from the top. Policing is demand-led from the bottom. Furthermore, the police have learned over the years how to meet this demand: they must therefore be allowed to get on with the job as they see fit, to police 'with discretion', above sectional interests and outside politics. Their autonomy from both politicians and the public is their virtue.

Against these arguments we would make four points. First, for cultural, ideological and organizational reasons the police exert a surprising degree of autonomy from both ruling elites and from the public. Second, the source of this autonomy lies in the peculiar contradictory class position and role that the police find themselves in. Third, a certain degree of autonomy is itself desirable, and the present degree and nature of such autonomy is a mixed blessing: it has both extreme drawbacks and comparative virtues. Finally, any attempt to change the nature of policing has to make central to its considerations the nature, extent and limits of police autonomy.

First, let us detail the sources of this autonomy. All bureaucracies maintain a certain variable distancing from the political instructions of those in control. This 'bureaucratic displacement of goals', as it is called, is commonplace in all organizations. It occurs, of course, within police forces. However, it is not this simple phenomenon that we are concerned with, but rather the peculiar nature of the autonomy of the police, as it relates to *public demand* on the one side, and to *policy-makers* on the other. Let us look at the three bases of this autonomy.

The Cultural Basis of Police Autonomy

'From the outset it was a deliberate policy to recruit men who had not the rank, habits, and station, of gentlemen. (Critchley 1978)

The police force is an extraordinary profession in that, since its inception, its membership has always been purposely recruited overwhelmingly from the lower classes. In *Blue-Coated Worker* (1978) Robert Reiner showed that 60 per cent of recruits came from working-class backgrounds and a further 17 per cent from the lower middle class. Only 5 per cent of recruits had university degrees, and there was no great statistical significance between the class origins of those in the ranks and those in supervisory positions. Even if we allow for the fact that commissioners and chief constables may come from middle-class backgrounds, the profession is characterized by an extraordinary lower-class homogeneity. Compare it, for example, with the caste-like character of the armed services, or the overwhelmingly middle-class professions of law, medicine and the established Church.

Such a force, then, has strong background links with the working class and only very fragile knowledge of or links with the upper orders. It deals primarily with working-class crime – both in protecting working-class people from crime and in regulating working-class behaviour. The focus of policing within the working class is largely upon the lower strata, towards whom the 'respectable' working class shows a certain degree of disdain. Yet the police, of course, deal with offences and infringements within the working class as a whole. Thus, given the likely effects of the resulting stigmatization among the respectable working class, the police pose a threat to self-esteem and respectability. They are therefore disliked by the poorest of the working class, but viewed with a contradictory mixture of respect and suspicion by the majority – and in particular by those sections of the working class from which they themselves are recruited, and in whose interests they see themselves, in the vast majority of instances, to be acting. The police, in short, are the organized super-ego of the respectable working class.

Although there is a reluctance to form close social relations with the police, to provide information on a completely voluntary basis – for at worst, it could be dangerous, and at best, a court appearance is time-consuming – this is scarcely the basis of a police state. The police are neither alienated from the working class, nor a part of it. Rather, our super-ego analogy points to the social basis of their autonomy: on the one hand a distancing by suspicion from the working class, and on the other, in their concern with working-class conceptions of law and order, a distancing from some at least of the concerns of policy-makers and legislators. The focus on lower-working-class street crime rather than crime in the workplace, the turning of a blind eye or the reluctance to become involved in male violence against women in the home, are instances of this.

Such autonomy can be both progressive and reactionary. It can purposely shield certain sections of the poor from the dispassionate impact of law; it can, on the other hand, be blatantly prejudiced and discriminating towards women, ethnic minorities and marginalized sections of the working class – the unemployed, gypsies, 'problem' families and so on. This cultural autonomy of the police from upper- and middle-class concerns undermines the strict application of bourgeois standards, while at the same time it mirrors and exacerbates reactionary tendencies within the working class itself. The police neither reflect nor meet the demands of the community as a whole, nor do they pursue the straightforward interests of their masters.

The Organizational Basis

We have indicated how, for reasons of logic and limited resources, police discretion is a necessity. The general rules of the lawyer or policy-maker and the dictates of chief constables must be translated on the ground by the rank and file police officer. It is this conceptual and material problem that provides the basis for police autonomy. But there are further, organizational, reasons which reinforce this autonomy. Chief among these is the peculiar position between the public and the state in which the police operate. On the one hand they are primarily involved in reactive rather than proactive work, responding to public demand. On the other, they are bound by a system of laws and regulations and instructed to maintain the Queen's Peace. They are, in other words, constrained by state instructions, but the focus of their concerns is the result of incessant public demand. Such a process affords a significant degree of *public* discretion – in deciding what crimes to report to the police. It is scarcely surprising, therefore, that the allocation of police time is determined by a mixture of public pressure and the concerns of the police themselves, particularly where the two overlap.

The Ideological Basis

The ideological notion of the political neutrality and operational responsibilities of the chief constable considerably affects the balance of power between public demand, which is immediate and pressing, and state demands, which are general and operationally non-immediate. This relative autonomy of the police, balanced as they are between the public and the state, allows the police considerable manoeuvrability and resistance to the demands of the latter, and is celebrated in an ideology of technicism: the police task is the purely technical one of law enforcement, and therefore is justly distanced both from the demands of the state – except insofar as laws are made by the state – and from the particular day-to-day concerns of the public. This philosophy of the essentially technical and apolitical nature of policing is enshrined, for example, in the 1964 Police Act, which underpins the operational autonomy of the chief constable from local authority control and, in England and Wales, gives one third of the seats on the police committees of local authorities to magistrates.

In order to transform the police into an agency that serves the mass of the population, fundamental changes have to be made in two related fields: in the information fed into policing from both the public and the state, and in the nature of political control exerted by public and state. Such changes will not eliminate a measure of discretion in police work – this would be both impossible and undesirable. Rather, it will more closely focus and delimit this necessary expression of autonomy. It is essential, therefore, that there should be two bodies mediating between the relationship of the police and that of the outside world. On the level of local police–public relations there should be a police authority consisting of a democratically elected public body – a subcommittee of the elected local authority to whom the police are accountable not only in matters of finance and expenditure but also in general policing strategy for the area. At the state level, in addition to direct accountability and control exercised by the Home Office, there should be a new office of public prosecutor. Finally, there must be a very specific relationship between the police and other social agencies such as social work, education, and housing departments of local authorities. In the remainder of this chapter we shall elaborate the general structure, and in

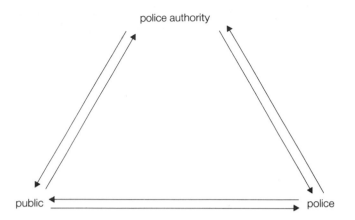

Figure 7   The tripartite relationship between police, police authority and public.

the last chapter we shall characterize the new style of policing which we advocate as compatible with this institutional framework.

The Local Accountability of the Police

The structure of local police accountability that we advocate can be described in terms of the tripartite relationship between the police, the police authority, and the public, as shown in Figure 7. The starting-point for this structure is our assumption of the inextricable relationship between accountability, public support and efficiency. Without accountability the vicious circles, described in Chapter 2, of declining flow of information to the police from the public and declining police efficiency cannot be broken. For it is only through the accountability of the police to the local political system that public confidence in them can be increased, and with it, the flow of information. In setting up the local community liaison panels under the 1984 Police and Criminal Evidence Act, the police and the Home Office have conceded that without public support the flow of information cannot, indeed, be improved. But, as we have argued, these local panels are not representative, nor, in the absence of police accountability, do they give the public any incentive to participate in the debate about policing priorities. The public will start to trust the police when it has a real influence over the policy-formation process at a local level. When it starts to trust the police it will increase the flow of information about crime. An increased flow of information about crime will permit increases in the clear-up rate and the abandonment of those items of police strategy, documented in preceding chapters, which are counterproductive in the fight against crime. This is the simple connection between account-ability and efficiency. Let us now analyse it in more detail.

The Public and the Police Authority

Police authorities in England and Wales are subcommittees of local government, usually of the county council or of the metropolitan county council (after abolition these latter will be replaced by joint boards). Two thirds of their members are elected councillors and one third are magistrates. In Scotland they are composed entirely of elected members. But, as we have seen, their ability to function as organs of police policy-making is non-existent. This situation must be changed. The police authority as the locally elected body must become the public voice of policing policy. While the police must neces-sarily retain their sphere of operational expertise in the detection of crime, chief constables and senior officers should be precluded from making *ad hoc* statements in policy matters which are not their proper or exclusive sphere of competence. (Thus the direct issuing of public statements to the media by the police would cease.) It is, of course, desirable that police representatives be coopted into the police authority. But elected members would predominate, and the decision-making role as regards the general policing strategy for the area would be theirs alone. Control by the police authority over the issuing of statements and information is important in a second respect –

it has a duty to educate and inform the public in matters of policing policy and crime prevention. It can do this by regularly conducting its own criminal victimization surveys, which would include the sampling of public evaluations of police efficiency. The results of such surveys and other information about crime and policing would be disseminated by the police authority, to assist the process of public debate on crime and policing priorities. It is the encouragement of public debate that is central. The more public debate about crime, the more competent the public will become at formulating and evaluating matters of policing policy, and the more rapidly will emerge a generation of local councillors, elected in the normal way, sitting on the police authority with a knowledge of both the needs of the public and of the methods and problems of policing the area.

The police authority would also have an important role to play in matters of crime prevention. The local authority rather than the police should manage Neighbourhood Watch schemes. Such schemes can have an important role in crime prevention if their methods of operation are accountable to the community as a whole. Thus the police authority could ensure that the 'best practice' was adhered to, and that politically acceptable criteria were being used – for example, in the reportage of 'suspicious circumstances' to the police.

Finally, the police authority would be the police complaints authority for the area. It would also ensure that any data collected in necessary surveillance exercises by the police was periodically 'weeded', and irrelevant information on private individuals removed from files or computers.

The Police and the Police Authority

The old tripartite arrangement under the 1964 Police Act has proved unworkable. The distinction between the responsibility of the *existing* police authorities (there is no police authority, save the Home Secretary, for the Metropolitan Police) and that of chief constables has proved unworkable. The distinction between 'maintaining an efficient force' – the responsibility of the police authority – and the control of all 'operational matters' by the chief constable, is an arbitrary one, as a number of commentators have, from time to time, pointed out, and as the 1984–5 miners' strike illustrated in graphic detail. Maintaining an efficient force – efficient, that is, in meeting public needs – demands the tailoring of general operational strategy to public need.

We therefore propose that the powers of the new police authorities include that of determining the general policing strategy for the area. We do not claim any originality in this proposal. Jack Straw attempted to introduce a Private Members' Bill into the House of Commons containing such proposals as long ago as 1979. The general policing strategy which the new police authority will issue will include the usual items referring to resources, recruitment, appointments and so on, but will also specify the crime profile for the area both geographically and in terms of types of crime from which different sections of the local community are suffering. The information for this profile will come from a number of sources: police reports to the police authority of the type of telephone and other calls for assistance they are receiving from the public, discussions in community liaison panels and in community groups, and discussions in the council chamber of the local authority informed by the police authorities' criminal victimization surveys. Finally, the strategic plan will outline the general methods whereby the police are to deal with crime. This will, of course, be based on a careful scrutiny of police methods and clear-up rates over the preceeding period. The police themselves will be able to offer their experience and advice and present their recommendations to the police authority through coopted members, and at the same time the results of their discussions with different community groups in the local liaison panels will be taken note of.

The strategic plan will include clear criteria for the circumstances under which particular types of operation may be used in the locality – such as surveillance if, for example, a large number of suppliers of dangerous drugs are believed to be operating in the area. The plan will also make plain the criteria which the police should use in responding to calls for assistance. The public will have had a chance to discuss such criteria in local liaison panels and in councillor's 'surgeries', and, of course, will have been able to elect councillors sympathetic to their views. The police authority will also, as mentioned, issue guidelines for the operation of crime prevention schemes such as Neighbourhood Watch. The police will provide the police authority with crime figures in the usual way, and these figures will be published by the authority, with accompanying analysis, as part of the annual report. In this way the exaggeration or misinterpretation of crime statistics which has occurred in recent years when they have been issued by the police themselves, especially in London, can be avoided. It should.be absolutely clear that certain matters will be outside the powers of a police authority. There will be no powers to give the chief constable directions in any individual case. The question of the confidentiality of information must be respected under the normal obligations of local authorities. Finally, the police authority will appoint chief officers of police. Again, this will act to counter a recent trend in which the Home Office appears to be increasingly interfering with existing police authority appointments.

The Police and the Public

In our conception, the most important direct relationship between the police and the public will be that in which the police respond to public calls for assistance. This will be discussed in the next chapter. These *immediate* demands for reactive policing complement the police authority's more general policy demands.

In addition, there is an important role in the new structure for the existing community liaison panels. They will, of course, be supplementary to the overall determination of policing policy by local government, so will be able to become focuses for specific types of consultation between different sections of the community and different sections of the police. The ultimate aim of community liaison will be to assist the police authority in formulating its general strategy and to assist the police in identifying particular problems. While the general determination of policing policy can only be sanctioned through the local political system based on universal suffrage, there is an important role for a type of dialogue which will ensure that the voices of all sections of the community, however small, are represented. These liaison groups could involve a variety of representatives, including teachers and social workers; and community groups with a crime-prevention element in their work could discuss problems with police officers in a very different atmosphere from that characteristic of the multi-agency policing portrayed in Chapter 6. Local community groups and trade unions, and groups with special policing needs, could discuss their problems with different groups of police officers. Women's groups could discuss problems arising from the police approach to the sexual harassment of women in public places, and male violence against women in the home. Specialist rape squad officers led by experienced women police would be especially involved in such discussions. Likewise, traffic division officers – though there is a strong case for civilizing many aspects of traffic control – could discuss with tenants' groups or residents living near main roads such issues as enforcing traffic laws against heavy vehicles and introducing bus lanes into the area. Likewise, ethnic minority groups would be able to discuss in detail the problem of racial attacks and the techniques by which the police were dealing with them.

Such consultation groups would be very different from the current community liaison panels. They would have a special role in breaking down the isolation of the police occupational culture. The dialogue would not just be with the police as a whole, but with particular groups of officers who were special-izing in particular community needs. These officers would then begin to develop some identification with community problems and see the point of view of community members. At the same time rank and file police officers could – since such dialogues would not be part of some bureaucratic police–public relations exercise – speak freely about the strains and problems that faced them in their particular work areas. The public would in this way be drawn closer to an understanding of the police point of view. There would, we hope, be a mutual understanding and a breaking down of entrenched positions. The police would become less isolated, and the public would be more trusting and sympathetic. This would have a pay-off in terms of increased information flow. Also it would, in the long run, be instrumental in changing the balance of police recruitment. Ethnic minorities would feel less reluctant to join the police, and women police officers would feel less isolated in taking up problems of sexism within the force.

We are well aware that all blueprints for anything other than what already exists can be labelled utopian, and a thousand and one rationalizations produced by people with 'experience' as to why such proposals are unworkable. We have tried to portray the direction in which the local admini- stration of policing must move if the crisis is to be resolved. What is most definitely utopian is the expectation that current policies will lead to anything other than a worsening situation.

The Police and Central Government

National legislation, of course, defines the range of illegalities which it is the job of the police to combat. And a second limitation on the autonomy of police discretion should come from the office of the Public Prosecutor. This office should be used to decide not only on the strength of evidence in particular cases, but on the desirability of public funds being spent on particular classes of offence. The office should have real political muscle and be willing to refer back to the police a sizeable number of cases, on the grounds that prosecution would be a waste of limited public resources and/or that discretion should be shown in order to do justice in individual cases.

The provision of a *national* system of public prosecution with clear policy guidelines, accountable to Parliament through the Attorney-General, would counterbalance any substantively unjust inconsistencies in enforcement between different police authority areas. At local level, national prosecution guidelines would require sensitive interpretation, necessitating close liaison between police authorities and regional Crown prosecutors. But at the same time a distinct separation of powers would have to be maintained between the two institutions. Prosecution guidelines established at national level would be closely geared to information provided by the police and other social control agencies. The police would make information available to central government in the same way as to the local police authority. In both cases such information would be scrutinized more closely and more formally than at present – that is, more in the fashion in which accountants analyse company reports or the Audit Commission analyses local government expenditure. Police statistics should be systematically compared with local crime surveys and carefully analysed from the standpoint of national prosecution policy. This would be a very different situation from the present, in which once a year the police issue the figures of rising crime, which are duly met with dismay in government and media, whereupon the police are summarily congratulated and granted further autonomy and resources, and told to get on with the job.

As part of this process of bringing police efficiency under closer national as well as local scrutiny, immediate steps should be taken to dismantle the unelected and wholly undemocratic decision-making processes developed by the Association of Chief Police Officers. ACPO's role in mobilizing and controlling the National Reporting Centre during the miners' strike of 1984–5 justifiably provoked considerable anxieties concerning the *ad hoc* creation of a national police force headed by a self-appointed caucus. Any decisions in such situations should be under full parliamentary control, and we would advocate the creation of a standing committee of the House of Commons to monitor and take responsibility for the implementation of policy. Chief constables would thus be directly accountable to Parliament where matters of national importance were concerned. Such matters might include the transportation of nuclear waste, anti-terrorist measures, or measures to stem the importation of heroin.

The Police and Other Agencies of Social Control

In our discussion of multi-agency policing in Chapter 6, we stressed the internal and external constraints on the work of other agencies to which close cooperation with the police in some of the ways envisaged by current government thinking would most likely lead. The democratic control of policing by elected police authorities would not necessarily prevent the blurring of boundaries between the police and other agencies whose work had a crime-prevention aspect. It therefore seems necessary to assert, in addition to the principle of democratic control, that of the separation of powers. In other words, a clear division between the work of the police and that of other agencies must be maintained. In terms of police work this will be elaborated in the next chapter. What is important to understand is that different agencies operate in very different ways, and that this would remain the case even under a system of greater local democracy than exists at present. The only acceptable sort of multi-agency policing is the separate and equal model discussed in Chapter 6. Even that would not escape certain general problems inherent in the preventive approach to crime (see pp. 115–17). The exchange of ideas and experiences between institutions is useful, but should be kept quite distinct from joint activity. Nevertheless, some joint projects would be necessary and joint access to data would be involved: for example, as mentioned in Chapter 6, police assistance to housing authorities in handling racial attacks on council estates. Any coordination and joint planning should be at the level of the local government bodies concerned: the police authority and the housing authority.

There is another reason for keeping the work of the police and other agencies separate, even where the police are subject to democratic control. A 'seamless web' of social control can emerge even in a democratic society, if it is not understood that there are certain irresolvable tensions in human existence that social policy-making cannot overcome. One such is that between free will and determinism. Police are, and should remain, very clearly rooted in the 'free will' end of the spectrum. That is to say, their job is to ask in any particular case: 'Was an offence committed? Who was responsible?', and act accordingly. Social workers will be concerned much more with the determinism end of the spectrum: 'What were the circumstances which led to the events, and what measures can be taken to avoid a recurrence of the situation?' One agency is concerned with law enforcement, and the other with treatment.

The point is that these two perspectives cannot be synthesized. A simple example will suffice. Police may advocate taking a child into care because she is always running away from home and committing offences, and police time is continually being used to track down the child and deal with the offences. The social worker concerned may oppose a care order from the perspective of the likely effect on the child and the family. The social worker may have spent several months working with the family to produce a situation in which the child no longer leaves home and a care order at this point may jeopardize several months' patient work. There are a myriad similar examples which experienced police officers and social workers will be able to point to, and which cannot be solved from the standpoint of some synthetic multi-agency philosophy, but only by conflict and compromise between the agencies involved. For such conflict and compromise to have anything like a reasonable outcome, the agencies must have equal power and involvement and be committed to their own standpoints.

This discussion brings us to the question of the boundaries to, and characterization of, the kind of police work that we see as compatible with the preservation of effective civil liberties and with growing public support.

9

Minimal Policing:
The Theory and Practice of a
Democratic Force

In earlier chapters we have argued that the failure of the police to control relatively mundane crimes and offences underlies much of the crisis in British policing. We have argued that there has been a real increase in reported crime, especially as it affects working-class people, but that this has been accompanied by a relative decrease in the flow of information between public and police. We have suggested that on the one hand this reduced flow of information has been used to justify a redefinition of policing, which has included the development of quasi-military units, surveillance and intelligence systems and increasingly widespread powers to detain and interrogate. On the other hand, we have seen the reverse response in the form of a public relations exercise which distances the police from crime investigation, and asserts the irrationality of a misplaced fear of crime on the part of the public. Here the responsibility for 'trivial' or 'secondary' crimes is hived off from the police and, in effect, thrown back upon those sections of society who have the greatest need for responsive and effective policing.

The claims made by the police in support of these developments are not, however, without a kernel of truth that accords with everyday experience. The inadequate flow of information from public to police underpins and gives substance to police claims that they can do little about most burglaries and street crime. We have to recognize the claims of the judiciary and the police that even in the most serious offences, and in situations where one might reasonably expect people to exhibit the most concern and come forward to 'help the police with their inquiries', all too often this just does not happen.

For example at the time the House of Lords was debating the provision of police powers of detention and stop and search for Scotland (29 January 1980), Lord Wheatley reminded the House of a particularly brutal murder in which three youths kicked a man to death in full view of a crowd of people leaving a bingo hall: 'Of all the mass of people the only person who intervened and the only person who was prepared to come forward and give evidence was a young married woman aged 21. The rest of the citizens did not want to become involved.' During his speech Lord Wheatley spoke repeatedly of the 'unwillingness of people to become involved' and how, in consequence, the police were 'constantly faced with the difficulties of getting evidence'. It is, he said, a 'tremendous problem . . . What are the difficulties of the police? They are many. But may I tell your Lordships that my experience so far as witnesses are concerned as they have appeared before me in the courts of Scotland is that the two chronic diseases are not heart trouble or lung cancer, they are myopia and amnesia.'

Lord Wheatley's view of things from the bench should not be dismissed out of hand. If there is a widespread reluctance among the public to help the police, it must not be put down to social irresponsibility or irrationality. Chief constables, for example, are fond of claiming a widespread fear of 'hardened criminals taking reprisals' against members of the public who give evidence to the police. While on occasion such things do happen, there is no doubt that the claim is exaggerated, but given the low clear-up rate, perhaps the fear is not altogether misplaced.

Where we would disagree with people like Lord Wheatley is in their belief that the way to counter this problem is to give the police increased powers of detention, interrogation and idenitfication – the philosophy of extending the coercive powers of the police to deal with the lack of public cooperation, which was adopted wholesale in the Criminal Justice (Scotland) Act 1980 and the Police and Criminal Evidence Act (1984) for England and Wales. As we have argued, such developments, taken alongside the increased use of surveillance and criminal intelligence collection, only make the problems worse. They intensify and give a further twist to the vicious circle of police–public alienation.

What is needed is a realistic alternative that does not rely on compulsion, detention, interrogation and surveillance to obtain information about crime, but that recognizes that unless the public provide information to the police, then the latter are powerless to do anything about crime. In the previous chapter we argued that the democratic accountability of policing to local government police authorities is a crucial part of such an alternative system. We have emphasized the role of the public and how a system of proper accountability would increase public willingness to yield information necessary to the solution of crime. But this does not mean that the police themselves have an any less central role in the investigation of crime. Information must be collected, interpreted, sifted and acted upon. The theory of 'minimal policing' which we elaborate in this chapter is an attempt to characterize a style of policing under a system of democratic accountability in which information is freely given by the public and where the police are sufficiently trusted to do the job they are paid for – the full and proper investigation of crime. Minimal policing is thus a style of policing that is not only precluded from using, but has *no generalized need for*, the extended use of surveillance, criminal intelligence, special units, powers of stop and search or the extended detention of witnesses and evidence; nor need it assimilate the work of other agencies to the police task.

The insistence on democracy and the collective account-ability of the police clearly distinguishes minimal policing from the market model of the New Right. Indeed, both the market model and the liberal–constitutionalist model exhibit a woeful inability to appreciate the sociological reality of police work and organization; the one permits an artless trust in atomized individualism and the other, a naive legalism. Minimal policing starts from a realistic appreciation of the problems of crime and policing, and is geared to the effective enforcement of the law and the efficient investigation of crime, yet retains a full commitment to the protection of individual rights and democratic freedoms as essential prerequisites of that objective. The strategy rests on a series of interrelated propositions: namely, maximum public initiation of police action and maximum access to the police, and minimal police-initiated action and minimum use of coercion. This is to be achieved through a combination of legal, political and organizational changes.

Maximum Public Initiation of Police Action

The first point to be made is that any effective system of policing must be geared to maximizing the voluntary input of the public and, by the same token, to keeping police coercion to the absolute necessary minimum. We have seen that in the vast majority of crimes that are cleared up, success has come about as a direct consequence of the public intervening and informing the police. In this sense, public initiation of police action is the key to effective policing. We have seen that where the police have attempted to take over this role and have laid claim to and built up their own data banks, the results have been nothing but a waste of money and police time (as with the Thames Valley force), to say nothing of the offence to civil liberties and the resulting atmosphere of distrust.

At the same time, however, the role of the police remains crucial. The information that members of the public have is frequently wild, misinformed and unreliable. One of the major functions of the police is therefore to establish what solid information is available and to examine and collect evidence in particular cases – in other words, to investigate crime very much with an eye to the courts and the laws of evidence and procedure, which, if properly formulated, should function as a significant control over police activity in this field (Baldwin and Kinsey 1985).

From this point of view, then, the objective of maximum public initiation of police action is not simply to provide the police with information. Nor is it to encourage a belief in 'self-policing' by the community or by individuals – a strategy which would bring the inherent dangers of unregulated militias and vigilante groups. Rather, crime must be investigated by the police with the public initiating action at two levels. First, at the collective level, the local police authority must establish, through the democratic process, the general guidelines for the exercise of police discretion and the priorities for the area. Second, at the individual level, the public shall request police assistance. Here the decision to involve the police in a particular matter, in by far the majority of cases, is best left to those immediately concerned. For example, if a fight in a pub is resolved amicably and neither party sees fit to call the police and press assault charges, then there is no reason why the police should be involved, unless somebody else – the landlord or a local resident, for example – wants, *as a victim of the offence*, to make a complaint. It should not be assumed as a matter of course that the police are best placed to decide how such incidents should be dealt with; it is often better for those involved to initiate any action. Too often in such cases, decisions taken by the police turn not on considerations of local need or public demand but on police-defined conceptions of what is in the public interest or – and for the police this often amounts to the same thing – what is in the police interest.

We would stress, however, that the conception of the public initiation of police action that we employ is not restricted to the individual complaint, as in the market model of policing. The collective level of initiation through police authority policy-making is of equal importance. There may, for example, be cases where a specific type of offence has given rise to public concern, yet individual calls on the police are not forthcoming. As we saw earlier, in cases of domestic violence, for example, the tendency with the 'police definition' of the situation is frequently *not* to intervene. Indeed, the existing forms of community–police liaison may increase that tendency, with police attitudes and priorities being reinforced by the voices of particular sections of the community – or what the police themselves define as the 'prevailing community opinion'. As Tony Faragher (1985) points out, 'Violence against women is clearly not the concern of "hard" models of policing. Within the "soft" model, with its accent on change by community consent and the avoidance of the use of legal means of enforcement where possible, battered women will be unlikely to find any enhanced protection from violence or effective legal redress' (p. 122). The interests of battered women may be more effectively represented in a democratic local political system, and in the type of liaison and discussion between community groups and the police that we outlined in the previous chapter. This may result in specific instructions originating in police authority policy as to procedure in such cases. Other changes, also hinted at in the previous chapter, such as the widening of police recruitment and the creation of special units, will be crucial in creating a police force prepared to treat domestic violence as seriously as many other offences.

What is entailed, therefore, in the concept of maximum public initiation of police action, is the collective action of police authorities and the individual action of victims and complainants. The consequence will be a minimization of the autonomy of police occupational culture and political attitudes in the drawing up of criteria for deciding when to intervene and when not to.

Minimum Necessary Coercion by the Police

The introduction of powers of detention and interrogation and of stopping and questioning suspects in the streets signals an emphasis in information-gathering by the British police on *police*-initiated action. Here it is essential to recognize that the manner in which information is obtained by the police is critical to the nature of policing itself. And the methods employed may be seen to range across a continuum from reliance upon voluntary statements, through compulsory powers of interrogation and covert intelligence collection, to the use of police spies and *agents provocateurs*. As such methods are routinely employed, the style of policing may be said to range from what is conventionally termed policing by consent to the methods of the police state.

Minimal policing, with the emphasis on public initiation, thus presents a radical form of policing by consent. The public are not being asked to place blind faith in 'police expertise', nor are they 'obliged to cooperate' for fear of the consequences. Minimal policing entails a strict limit on police powers, working from the premise that it is for the police to cooperate with and respond to the demands of the public, rather than vice versa. Thus legislation such as the Police and Criminal Evidence Act 1984 and its Scottish predecessor approaches the whole question of crime investigation from a position diametrically opposed to that of minimal policing. Where minimal policing encourages and relies upon evidence freely brought forward by witnesses and victims of crime, the new legislation clearly places the emphasis of police work upon the compulsory interrogation of suspects with the intention of obtaining confessions.

Some 25,000 persons are detained every year for interrogation under the Criminal Justice (Scotland) Act 1980, over half of whom are released without charge. An equivalent figure for England and Wales would be in excess of a quarter of a million. As has been seen with the Diplock Courts in Northern Ireland, where these methods are pursued to their logical conclusion, such powers are frequently accompanied by a weakening of due process. This is already evident in the readiness of the judiciary both in Scotland and in England

and Wales to relax the laws of evidence and the judges' rules, and to allow evidence which some years ago would have been ruled inadmissible (Baldwin and Kinsey 1982, chapter 5).

Minimal policing thus entails a profound respect for civil liberties, but not only on the grounds of liberal principle. Respect for the rights of the individual, as embodied in the two principles of maximum public initiation of police action and minimum necessary coercion, is one of the most effective guarantees of an efficient and socially just system of policing.

The demand for maximum public initiation and for a radical version of policing by consent does not, however, ignore the fact that policing is, by its very nature, coercive. The police are different from other agencies of social control in that in certain circumstances they can, and do, engage in the legitimate use of violence in pursuit of their goals. In making an arrest, for example, the police are permitted at law to use 'reasonable force'. The use of such force by the police in performance of their duties is quite proper, so long as those duties are precisely stated at law and there are effective means of obtaining redress in case of the abuse of power. Many of the problems to be faced in current legislation, though, stem from the fact that the duties of the police are imprecisely defined, such that the powers bestowed on them are, in effect, discretionary powers, which turn to such an extent on the subjective judgement of the individual police officer that they are beyond effective review by the courts and thus 'above the law' (Baldwin and Kinsey 1985).

The legislative framework of minimal policing would seek, first, to define the limits of minimum necessary coercion; second, to define the precise extent of police powers of intervention and interference in private lives and liberty, and reduce the scope of police discretion; and third, to minimize the role of police-initiated activity while maximizing that of the public. Thus if the police are to be recognized as an agency which includes, inevitably, coercion among its powers, not only must those powers be precisely limited and defined, but the legal powers and organizational objectives of the police must be clearly distinguished from those of other social control agencies – such as social work, for example.

Minimal Police Intervention

It follows, therefore, from the two principles we have discussed, that one practical objective of minimal policing must be a severe contraction of coercive and covert police intervention in public and private life. The proper function of police is the investigation and detection of crime, and at present the police are ineffective and inefficient in doing this. But the use of extended coercive powers and of techniques of surveillance and intelligence is both objectionable in itself and self-defeating. The police have become too intrusive in daily life. They decide when and in what circumstances to intervene; when to act in industrial disputes, whom to place under low-level surveillance, and which sections of the population are a threat both to others and to themselves. The police have become too diverse and pervasive. They have, as John Alderson advocated, 'penetrated society'. Increasingly they are interfering in aspects of both public and private life that, socially and politically, are none of their business.

So our concept of minimal policing is, in many respects, opposed to the ideas of John Alderson, by many regarded as a liberal and progressive thinker on policing matters. Where we argue for minimal intervention, Alderson argues for maximum penetration. Further, Alderson's proactive approach to policing envisages a high degree of cooperation with other agencies of social control, both local and central. Minimal policing sees the police as offering a particular service subject to direct public control. The most radical difference between our view and that of Alderson lies in the priority that he gives to the social-work role of the police. Whereas minimal policing recognizes that the police can and do play a useful role as a referral agency, proactive policing, as advocated by Alderson, amounts to an almost total integration of the police and the social services: '[proactive policing] requires an approach to social problems adumbrating crime, disorder, or social agitation of one kind or another together with social services, health, welfare, probation, employment, social security, housing, planning, and other statutory and voluntary services. Removing criminogenic social conditions is its objective' (Alderson 1985, p. 39). Divorced from all connection with current political and economic reality, such ideas have a superficial attraction. Were such a society a realistic option, it would be about as liveable-in as *Brave New World*, but in the present conditions of economic crisis and mass unemployment it remains sheer fantasy.

For once, it is difficult to disagree with Sir David McNee (Commissioner of the Metropolitan Police before Sir Kenneth Newman), who wrote in 1979 that, while he was 'not one to shirk trouble', such issues 'are questions of social justice and a matter for local and national government. Their solution does not lie within the remit of the police' (McNee 19799, p. 83). The point is well made, for in effect McNee is arguing the case for a strict separation of institutional power and responsibility. This is particularly important if we consider the practical implications of proactive policing. For, in the present social and economic conditions, the only real opportunity for proactive policing is in individual cases, that is, in private lives, where, to all intents and purposes, police work becomes social work and social work becomes police work. As we have argued in an earlier chapter, both police and social work have fundamental roles to play as social control agencies. What is absolutely essential to both, however, if they are to remain effective, is that their roles be kept quite distinct, both politically and insitutionally. The absorption of any part of the work of the one by the other only serves to undermine the credibility and efficiency of both. Indeed, many agencies have a social-control aspect to their work, and have had so for a long time without – until recently – encountering the suggestion that their relationship with the police should take any other form than calls for assistance in the last resort.

As the PSI report put it, the police have a 'limited yet decisive' role to play in the control of behaviour. The report mentions two examples illustrating this. The Gas Board has an elaborate procedure for dealing with customers who do not pay their bills, in which the actual disconnection of supply, the final sanction, is applied in a very small number of cases, and only in 5 per cent of these is a police officer likely to be involved. The second example is the control of disruptive behaviour in schools:

Many fights and scuffles take place in schools which might in other circumstances be interpreted as minor assaults. There is also a considerable amount of damage to school property (most of it minor damage) and a fair number of thefts. The schools have their own systems of rewards and punishments for trying to prevent this kind of behaviour and dealing with it when it does occur . . . The vast majority of fights, thefts and incidents involving deliberate damage to property are dealt with by school procedures and within the family. There is always, implicitly, a threat that a matter may be reported to the police if the offender does not step into line, but in practice the police are informed in a very small number of cases (though we do not know what the proportion is) . . . Thus schools and families not only bear the main responsibility for controlling the behaviour of children, *but they also largely decide* when the police shall be involved and whether or not formal proceedings shall be started. (PSI 1983, vol. 1, p. 12 our emphasis)

Thus many of the ingredients of minimal policing, though by no means all, are to be found in existence and are now under threat from newer conceptions of multi-agency and proactive policing.

Our argument, we believe, will accord with the gut-level response of many police officers concerning what is 'police work'. As we have said, social policy and social work should be kept separate from the policing task, which must be precisely defined as the investigation and control of crime.

Police are neither sufficiently qualified nor sufficiently dispassionate to get involved in other areas.

Clearly, the introduction of minimal policing, with its emphasis on the public initiation of police action, will require the complete reorganization of police work – more complete than simply putting officers back on the beat. Some indication of the extent of the necessary reorganization can be gleaned by considering how little of their time the police actually spend 'fighting crime'. Recent Home Office research shows, for example, that, on average, in a divisional police station in England and Wales only 15 per cent of a uniformed police officer's time – less than an hour and quarter in an eight-hour shift – is spent attending incidents in response to calls from the public. Of these approximately one third only are described as 'crime incidents'. The important finding here is not that so little crime is reported to the police, but that of the remaining working day the police officer will spend no more than an hour, and probably considerably less on crime investigation or follow-up work. Indeed, when the results of such studies as are available are carefully analysed, it seems that uniformed police officers spend as much time in the police canteen as they do out on the streets investigating crime. Thus the Merseyside Survey of Police Officers, conducted as part of the *Merseyside Crime Survey*, concluded:

The finding of the *Merseyside Crime Survey* that crime investigation and the provision of an emergency response are the public's highest policing priorities (see *MCS*, First Report, p. 45) contrasts markedly with the very small proportions of police time spent answering emergency calls (3 per cent) and interviewing suspects, witnesses and informants (6 per cent). [This is especially worrying] as interviewing members of the public and possible witnesses about the events under inquiry is generally regarded as the most efficient form of crime investigation.

Furthermore, the *MCS* also revealed that across Merseyside one in four respondents expressed some dissatisfaction with the police after reporting an offence. The main reasons for this were police inaction and failure to help (see *MCS*, First Report, p. 29). For the sake of both greater efficiency and public satisfaction it would appear that more time could be given over to initial response and the immediate investigation of offences as they are reported, without undue pressure on resources. To this end, it would be highly desirable to reduce the extent of administrative duties and clerical work which takes up almost a quarter of the divisional officers' time . . . [It] should be noted that of the time at present spent outside police premises, very little is given over to tasks related to crime investigation. In comparison with 'uncommitted' patrolling, this appears to be disproportionately low. That such activities should account for so little of police time can help neither clear-up rates nor public relations. (Kinsey 1984)

The amount of a patrol officer's time given over to 'preventive' or 'uncommitted patrolling' is in fact substantial: well over a third of the working day. Indeed, patrol work – whether on foot or by car – consumes more time and resources than any other job. Some 70 per cent of police manpower is employed in the uniform branch, over half of whom are employed on patrol work. The most recent estimates suggest that throughout England and Wales, but excluding London, 28,000 officers are deployed on patrol. It is interesting to note that, contrary to popular wisdom, there are in fact more officers employed in patrol work than in the early post-war period (Hough 1980, p. 7).

However, patrol work, as it is presently organized – especially on foot – is a dull, monotonous job which police officers regard more as a painful exercise than as a socially useful duty (Baldwin and Kinsey 1982; Jones 1980). Of the two, mobile patrol is much preferred. A car is at least warm, watertight and windproof, but – more important from the officer's perspective – the freedom and mobility of the panda car promises much more scope to seek out crime and catch criminals than does foot patrol. In reality, however, the chance that a patrol officer will stumble across a crime in progress is remote in the extreme. Nor is the preventive presence as effective as common sense might lead one to think. As the Home Office study pointed out, 'this is not surprising when one recognises that even in a busy sub-division only ten crimes a day will be reported to the police and many of these will occur in places inaccessible to police patrols' (Hough 1980, p. 11). Statistics are not available for this country, but in 1967 the President's Crime Commission in the United States estimated that a patrol officer in a large American city could expect to intercept a street robbery in progress only once every fourteen years.

In fact, almost invariably, the kind of offences picked up by patrolling officers are petty, 'self-reporting' offences such as drunkenness and rowdiness – occurrences which, as we have argued, are better left for public-initiated police action. Police intervention, then, is often born of boredom. Indeed, Jones (1980) reports his police colleagues' reaction to beat work, in which they describe the beat as a prison. In such conditions the routine employment of stop and search powers on suspicion is hardly surprising – if nothing else, it helps to relieve the tedium and may even provide an excuse to get back to the station. In other words, whether in car or on foot, 'preventive' patrols encourage police-initiated action. Police intervention in public life is indeed positively encouraged by the conditions of police work.

In part, therefore, the minimization of police intervention in public life can only be achieved by a fundamental restructuring of the working conditions of the uniformed patrol officer. This will inevitably have severe repercussions on other aspects of policing. Indeed, if efficient crime investigation is to become a reality, then clearly the palpable inefficiency of Criminal Investigation Departments (CID), shown up both by the PSI study of the Metropolitan Police and by the Merseyside Police Survey, must also be addressed.

These findings, coupled with the appalling clear-up rates achieved by the police in general and, more particularly in this context, the severely inhibiting and morale-damaging impact that specialization has had on the majority of uniformed police officers, lead us to advocate a radical reorganization of criminal investigation. Clearly there is a case for the development of specialist skills in some aspects of criminal investigation, as, for example, in complex company fraud and embezzlement, and in the handling of particular types of offences such as rape and domestic violence. But in general there is a strong case for returning the investigation of crime to uniformed officers and for cutting back the role of specialized crime investigation. This would result in the abolition of the CID as at present constituted and defined.

The advantages of such a move are self-evident. Criminal investigation would be regarded as a major, and indeed the most important, part of a police constable's work. Not only would job satisfaction and morale be immediately improved – officers would be engaged in 'real police work' – but also the local police officer would be visibly engaged in doing exactly what the public wants. In such circumstances public satisfaction with the police would be likely to rise, and there would be a far more efficient use of police resources, as the inordinate time spent in administration and paperwork could be significantly reduced.

On the same grounds there is a case for the abolition of special squads within the uniformed branch of the service, such as 'instant response units' and Special Patrol Groups. For example, the Merseyside Police Survey questioned whether the continued deployment of a separate 'Operational Support Division' (OSD) could be justified. At the time of the survey, officers of the Merseyside Operational Support Division were particularly heavily involved in policing industrial disputes (17 per cent of police time). Other special duties accounted for a further 8 per cent of their time. In comparison, officers in the territorial divisions spent 7 per cent of their time on all special duties (including industrial disputes).

This makes it all the more surprising that OSD officers were able to put in a remarkably high level of uncommitted patrol work (22 per cent) – a higher level than that recorded in the Divisions (18 per cent) and more than was spent at industrial disputes. This is perhaps understandable as on almost every other performance indicator – that is, except for time spent on other special duties – OSD officers seem to have substantially less to do than their colleagues. Thus, even at the height of the miners' dispute, the OSD does not appear to have been particularly stretched, although at that time these officers were working on average 1 hour 17 minutes overtime per day.

On the basis of these findings it is worth asking what is the precise role of the OSD, beyond offering general 'support' and a pool of officers available at all times for special duties and (relatively infrequent) industrial disorders. In comparison with other sections of the force, it would seem that the OSD is largely unproductive and under-worked. Crime investigation and prevention are clearly beyond the OSD officers' remit; they spend less time answering emergency calls than general patrol officers; they process fewer arrests and spend less time in court than their divisional counterparts; and they have virtually no informal contacts at all with the public.

Fundamental changes to police organization are necessary if police-initiated intervention is to be reduced in favour of crime investigation relying on public initiation. Thus the policy of minimal policing would seek to place a completely different emphasis upon the work of the uniformed officer. It would move away from the practice of random preventive patrols towards active crime investigation. This would result in officers being in more, rather than less, contact with the public, and so there is no reason to suppose that the capacity to respond to emergency 'treble 9' calls should in any way be impaired. Police would spend more time out on the streets and following up publicly initiated complaints, rather than finding ways to kill time and alleviate the boredom. The emphasis would be placed squarely on the investigation of actual offences rather than of potential offenders. It is therefore essential for the success of minimal policing to establish within the police forces a practice of what might be termed 'generic policing', which would lay stress on the general problems and purposes of crime investigation, thereby reversing the trend to ever more specialization.

This is just one of the objectives to be realized if, in practice, minimal policing is to provide a more effective means of crime control than the present bureaucratic, top-heavy approach,

the unintended consequence of which has been the institution-
alization of police harassment of certain sections of the public.
The object must be to structure police work so that it actively
encourages the investigation of crime, while actively discourag-
ing police-initiated action, thereby maximizing the opportunity
for, and benefits of, public initiation.

Maximum Public Access to the Police

The overall structure of police accountability to the public
and the role of police authorities was dealt with in the last
chapter. Such bodies would provide the essential element of
democratic control and a wider dimension to the public
initiation of policing. It is essential to minimal policing that
this be so for, if the policy is to be successful and the relative
decline in information flow from public to police is to be
reversed, then the need to make policy choices in the use and
allocation of limited resources becomes all the more critical.
Increased demand on the police will inevitably mean greater
selection and pressure in the use of those resources. In such
circumstances, the need for democratic resolution is crucial
and we would, therefore, seek extended powers, as we have
specified, for local police authorities to determine overall
policing policy and priorities within force areas. We would
stress, though, that this would not entail outright operational
or 'political' control of day-to-day matters by the police
authority. Such an option is both illogical and impractical, if
for no other reason than that, in general, the law inevitably
requires the exercise of discretion by police officers in particular
situations. This must remain so even when the blanket
discretionary powers such as those conferred on the police in
recent legislation are reduced to a minimum.

The need to establish priorities for the use of police time
and resources is illustrated by some of the findings of the
Merseyside Crime Survey (Kinsey, 1984). While it is neither
difficult nor controversial to establish priorities for crime

investigation for a police force as a whole, local variations and the different needs of particular areas or social groups produce a much more complex and often highly emotive situation. The survey showed clear agreement throughout the county that robberies with violence were a high priority (75 per cent of respondents felt this to be the case). Likewise, sexual assaults against women were rated as a priority by 73 per cent, and burglary by 68 per cent. It was, however, quite clear that there was far less agreement upon what the police should spend *least* time on. Thus the report concluded:

The results would seem to suggest that county-wide there is a clear set of immediate priorities in relation to crime – priorities with which it is unlikely that the police disagree. At the same time there is an equally clear need for very careful consultation at the local level to establish particular, if less urgent demands . . . In respect of responding to such localised variation and demands of relatively low priority, the lack of social contact between police and public in certain areas may be a significant factor. Indeed a failure on the part of the police to recognize local variation in low-level priorities may partly explain the large number of respondents who felt the police 'did not have a good understanding of the area.' (Kinsey, 1984, p. 48)

The central role of local police authorities in determining local needs is thus essential if public confidence and satisfaction with police provision is to be ensured. Only on such a basis can it reasonably be expected that information and cooperation from the public will be forthcoming. Without the adequate monitoring of police practice and without democratically agreed priorities, we may soon see realized the fears recently expressed by Selma James and Nina Lopez-James of the English Collective of Prostitutes, concerning the Sexual Offences Bill, when they wrote that 'the Bill is intended as a new 'sus' law against prostitute women and black and other working-class men . . . The Bill is using prostitution and moral prejudices to increase police control of the streets' (letter to the *Guardian*, 18 May 1985).

Insofar as the law would allow the police themselves to define and determine the needs and interests of local communities, such fears refer to a distinct possibility. On the other hand, it must also be said that in certain areas many women are harassed by male 'kerb-crawling'. Over half of the women in one inner-city area of Liverpool, for example, reported that they were 'very upset' by such behaviour during the last year. This is one reason, no doubt, why so many women simply do not go out of the house on their own at night. A properly formulated law prohibiting kerb-crawling could therefore be of benefit, provided there was a definite and demonstrable need for it and provided there was an effective mechanism for reviewing police action with regard to such a law.

It is clear, therefore, that we strongly disagree with those of the liberal centre and the *laissez-faire* right who would roll back the state and limit policing only to those 'serious' crimes of 'considerable' impact. A blanket policy of decriminalization can all too easily amount to a policing equivalent of the policy of decarceration which, in certain instances, leads only to the abandonment and decanting of those in need into society without support. We do not underestimate the profound injustices and biases of the criminal law as it is presently constituted and enforced, and there are particular areas in which we support calls for decriminalization, but many if not most offences on the criminal statutes are in fact socially offensive. It is difficult to conceive of any society in which personal theft, burglary, sexual assaults or personal violence would not be regarded as wrong in themselves. The problem we see in this respect is associated with the nature of punishment, and not with any lack of need for crime control or social censure. Thus, supposedly 'trivial' offences cannot be exempted from police attention. The man who hits his wife regularly must be as much within the orbit of state intervention as the violent bank robber.

Similarly, there is confusion over the category of 'crimes without victims', which ranges from areas such as marihuana-smoking which harms no one, through prostitution which may cause severe problems for a community, to the sale of heroin for injection which is pernicious in the extreme. In the latter case decriminalization would obviously be a retrograde step. The *laissez-faire* rhetoric of the Adam Smith Institute, which has prompted members of the Federation of Conservative Students to call for the decriminalization of heroin, forgets that the weak and the vulnerable are not equally free in the market-place. By all means let us roll back the state in those areas where its impact is detrimental – in the detention centres where young people commit suicide, in the long-term prisons and psychiatric hospitals where people are turned into vegetables, and, as we have argued throughout this book, in the illegitimate use of state violence wherever it occurs.

But the state can also protect. We have pointed to the protection of children and the policing of domestic disputes, which, with adequate legislation introduced and enforced, could and should be much more vigorous and thorough. If it is true that we must beware the 'extension of the net', we must also learn to distinguish between those interventions which needlessly harass and those which are genuine safety nets.

We also part company from the Wilson–Kelling hypothesis (see Chapter 4) so popular within Home Office research circles at present, in noting how the distinction – immensely influential in the literature on crime control – between order maintenance and social service functions is merely an academic embellishment of existing police working practices and definitions. Police culture may well rate a bank robbery as a 'real crime', while seeing the resolution of a domestic dispute as a mere social service function and not 'real police work', but we cannot accept the police's working definitions as the criterion for what should be done. As we have said earlier, if policing is to be ordered around the public interest, such distinctions will have to be radically reformulated. The appropriate criterion of police action is whether a crime has been or is about to be committed, and whether the public deems it worthy of police intervention. Police discretion is inevitable and vital, but it must be contained within publicly drawn parameters. When

events presently defined as within the area of 'order maintenance' are criminal, then and only then are they the proper
object of police attention. Those incidents which are strictly
'social service' are, on the other hand, matters for social
welfare agencies, not the police. The shedding of these concerns will greatly help the police to focus upon their prime and
sole task, that of crime control.

If we redefine the conventional distinction between crime
control and order maintenance by asserting that the real and
only legitimate basis of police intervention is the commission
of a crime or offence, the Wilson–Kelling hypothesis can be
reformulated to reveal an element of truth. We can thus agree
that the control of minor crime is, by and large, as important
as the control of major crime. Indeed, most crime is minor
crime in that it does not involve large sums of money or severe
injury. But for the vulnerable, as we have said, many minor
crimes are major, and the accumulation of many such offences
over time only compounds and emphasizes the fact. Thus the
maintenance of order, in the sense of policing acts of vandalism
or violent offences in the home or in the pub, is essential.
Where crimes are allowed to go unregulated, it is true, as the
Wilson–Kelling hypothesis suggests, that social order begins
to collapse. Whole sections of inner-city America substantiate
this.

There are, on the other hand, genuinely minor crimes such
as the possession of marihuana or some drunkenness offences
which trouble few people and are rarely a subject of public
complaint to the police, but in which the police intervene
regularly at the expense of hostility and alienation. There are
also activities which simply are not criminal – being out late at
night, carrying a bag down the street or standing on a street
corner – yet where the police intervene regularly for their own
reasons, which results in even greater indignation. In all such
circumstances the justification for police action must be the
needs and demands of the local populace, not merely what is
important in terms of police culture and their assumptions

about police work. Appropriate criteria should be established by the police committees but, even so, under no circumstances should the police ever intervene where there is no evidence of illegality. Police action of this sort does not produce what Wilson–Kelling would see as the maintenance of an informal order which facilitates crime control, but, on the contrary, it fundamentally undermines the community by creating the basis for crime and public alienation.

The Advantages of Minimal Policing

The strategy we have outlined in this chapter offers a coherent alternative to the programme of community policing offered by liberals such as John Alderson, and to the order-maintenance model of Wilson and Kelling (Chapter 4). It recognizes the priority which must be given to the fundamental problems of crime and differential victimization analysed in this book, but respects the equal priorities that must be given to civil liberties. It offers the basis for a radical reorganization of the police and a limitation on their powers, while providing for an efficient and effective system of policing in line with public needs. It rests upon the following propositions, established by solid research and widely recognized by both academics and practitioners.

1 The vast majority of crimes cleared up by the police are, in fact, those in which individual members of the public have provided the critical information and have initiated police action. Thus, by emphasizing public initiation we maximize that aspect of police work which is most effective.

2 Minimal policing encourages contact between the police and the public in those circumstances where cooperation is most forthcoming, that is, where police presence has been deemed necessary and desirable and has been requested. Conversely, it minimizes those instances which most clearly

undermine public confidence in the police – that is, where the police are seen to be 'interfering', or acting officiously or according to priorities derived from bureaucratic inertia or occupational culture rather than public need.

3 Minimal policing recognizes that selection and unevenness are an inevitable part of policing. 'Differential policing' – is unavoidable where there is pressure on time and resources in the criminal justice system. Minimal policing provides that such selection be made, in the first instance, by those who are most at risk – namely, the victims of crime – but within parameters set down by the democratically elected police authority.

4 Minimal policing emphasizes that policing is and should be about crime and law enforcement, and restricts police activity to this clearly defined area. In other words, it cuts out that whole ill defined grey area of 'pre-emptive policing' with its emphasis upon covert 'intelligence collection', surveillance and random stop and search. It also clarifies the role of the police officer, who is unambiguously defined as working in crime control and investigation rather than as a quasi-welfare worker. Thus the dangers of proactive policing and multi-agency policing are minimized.

5 Finally, within the concept of the public initiation of police action, minimal policing emphasizes the principle of democratic accountability and the protection of individual rights and civil liberties as an integral element of overall policing strategy.

We believe that, as well as offering a coherent *philosophy* of policing, minimal policing provides a practical basis for reform at local and national level.

At local level the emphasis of minimal policing is on the joint role of individual members of the public requesting police intervention and the police authority establishing local needs and priorities. Under the present legal framework, not only is there no police authority for Greater London – the Metropolitan Police are directly responsible to the Home Secretary – but the existing policing authorities in England and Wales and Scotland have little if any power to challenge the 'operational' policy decisions of their chief constables. The distinction established in the 1964 Police Act, whereby the police authorities are responsible for 'maintenance of an efficient force' and chief constables are responsible for all 'operational decisions', with the Home Secretary as a court of appeal in any conflict between the two and having a veto on decisions, effectively collapsed under the strain of policing the miners' strike of 1984–5. This dispute offered vivid illustrations both of the impossibility of maintaining an efficient force *without* control over 'operational' decisions that took large numbers of police officers outside the force area and away from normal duties at considerable financial cost, and of the role of the Home Office as effective veto over any attempt by police authorities to force some measure of accountability on their chief constables (for a detailed account see Spencer 1985).

At the same time, two other factors have recently helped to keep the debate about the powers of police authorities in public focus. First, in response to the miners' strike and the issues in policing organization that it highlighted, a number of senior police officers have called for the 'depoliticization' of policing by even further reducing the democratic element – powerless as it already is – in local police authorities. Among such senior officers are James Anderton, Chief Constable of Greater Manchester, and Ian Oliver, Chief Constable of Central Scotland. Ian Oliver, writing in *Police Review* (2 November 1984) under the title 'Independence and impartiality', recognizes that 'there are some genuine and perhaps understandable concerns within local government circles. Not surprisingly, the apparent ability of chief constables to spend large amounts of money at will – and to such an extent that other community services may be put at severe risk – has caused considerable alarm in many a council chamber.' But he is nevertheless concerned that 'some [police] authorities have abused their responsibilities for party-political purposes.' Oliver seems splendidly ignorant of the contradiction between, on the one hand, recognizing that there can be a question of deciding how to allocate scarce resources between police and other community services, and on the other hand denigrating as 'party-political' the main mechanism that democratic societies – by contrast with totalitarian societies of the right or of the left – have developed to deal with this problem. Oliver continues:

the idea of some appointed police authority members (other than magistrates), in addition to those who are elected, becomes very attractive and the example of selection in Northern Ireland offers a system worthy of consideration for the mainland. Clearly policing is a matter for 'political' consideration but the distinction must be between the 'partisan political interest' and that of the community. (*Police Review*, 2 November 1984)

The Northern Ireland police authority, as established under the 1970 Police Act (Northern Ireland), a prototype which Oliver and others wish to introduce on the mainland, is made up entirely of members who are *nominated* by the Secretary of State for the province. Such members are in a similar position to magistrates in the English police authorities.

The idea that the 'commuity interest' can be better repre-sented by individuals nominated rather than elected through the normal process of party-political conflict and debate is a familiar stock-in-trade of all forms of political authoritarianism. But it strikes a complementary note to the second factor current in the debate on police accountability: the Thatcher government's intended abolition of the metropolitan county councils. It is intended that the metropolitan counties' police authority functions will be vested in joint boards of one third magistrates and two thirds nominated members from the lower-tier district councils. While it is true that the nominat-ing bodies will be lower-tier elected councillors and not government ministers, as in Northern Ireland, the democratic element in police authorities will nonetheless be severely weakened. The joint board will cover the area of the police force – often coterminous with the large metropolitan councils due to be abolished – and the members nominated by the lower-tier councils may come from a diversity of political standpoints if there are different party majorities on the district councils. This will make it harder for the nominated members to pursue a coherent agreed policy on police matters – even with their limited powers – and will naturally strengthen the power of the magistrates on the joint board as well as giving the chief constable more effective autonomy on the board.

The effects of these changes, apart from launching a fundamentally undemocratic attack on the structure of local government, will devalue the experience which many of the larger metropolitan council police authorities have built up in recent years. Through conflicts with their chief constables over handling the urban disturbances of 1981 and, more recently over the miners' strike, these police authorities have been able to develop a body of expertise on police matters outside the control of the police themselves. The recent history of the Merseyside police authority provides a good example of elected councillors starting to 'ask the right questions' about policing. The authority has, for example, challenged the monopoly of knowledge and expertise asserted by senior police strategists, by commissioning their own research into the crime problems faced by the people of Merseyside.

The *Merseyside Crime Survey*, including the Survey of Police Officers, fell within the council's police budget and was funded up to 50 per cent by the Home Office. On the basis of these findings – many of which we have referred to in this book – the authority's statutory duty to 'maintain an adequate and efficient force' is given particular bite. The findings on the use of police time may justifiably prompt questions as to the value for money which present force organization provides for the area. The findings of the crime survey provide the basis for a public discussion of policing aims. Such initiatives pave the way for the democratization of police policy-making, and the availability of such information is a step forward within the existing system towards a proper public discussion of policing and crime.

The reforms we suggest are, of course, a matter for a future Labour government determined to tackle the problem of crime and its impact on working-class people. As Tory plans to abolish second-tier local government are carried through, such a Labour government will face the task of reconstructing the whole framework of democratic police accountability. In the meantime, at a local level, Labour councils can do much to emulate the role of such police authorities as Merseyside in 'asking the right questions' about policing, and helping to create a climate conducive to reform. For this reason we see it as important that local councils should aim to participate in the existing police–community liaison panels. We have already noted (Chapter 8) how these unrepresentative bodies can be used to undermine local government.

But the struggle for police accountability is not simply a question of particular forms of organization and consultation structures, but of the balance of political forces and public opinion over a period of time. Councils which refuse to participate – as some Labour councils have done – will create a framework in which the police and the Home Office, particularly in London where local government is powerless with regard to police matters, can build up their own expertise in public relations and in the development of community liaison panels as a powerful legitimizing system for policies that are decided by the central police bureaucracy with only a show of consultation. Local councils that do participate, however, can perform a vital leadership and educative role in such consultation panels which, ultimately, will strengthen the case for proper police accountability.

The police committees of local councils – powerless as they are in London – do have research and resource back-up from which to devise their own policing plans for the locality and conduct their own consultation exercises and social surveys. In this way councillors will build up their expertise on policing matters in the locality. They will then, in the consultation panels, be able to make clearly formulated proposals and demands upon the police, perhaps coordinating them with additional local publicity and joint action between boroughs. In such a way the case for proper police accountability is strengthened. If, for example, the police take little notice of coherent demands made by council representatives in consultation panels, then this will serve publicly to show the need for police accountability. If the police do act on the advice of councillors on major issues, this, again, will demonstrate the competence of the council as a policy-initiator in the policing field, and again strengthen the case for accountability. The crucial issue facing Labour borough councils, in London particularly, is not whether to have anything to do with the police–community liaison panels, but how to follow in the footsteps of provincial police authorities such as Merseyside and London boroughs like Islington which have taken seriously the question of policing policy in their localities.

In addition to the question of the reform of the relationship between police and local government, we believe that many of the reforms we suggest on police organization and work will be well understood by general patrol officers within the police, even if they are rejected at more senior levels. Serious arguments need to be addressed to the Police Federation in these respects. Such issues as we have raised will have a greater impact upon police officers' thinking than any amount of 'human awareness' training. A considerable amount of research has shown that many current aspects of police work – traffic control and involvement with the social services, for example – are disliked intensely by patrol officers. The emphasis we place on crime investigation will be well received. Likewise, a greater civilianization of clerical work and middle-management tasks will find little opposition.

At the level of law reform, minimal policing is wholly compatible with the arguments of civil libertarians who have opposed recent extensions of police powers in Scotland and England and Wales. It is essential to minimal policing that such extensions are repealed and that new statutory provisions are introduced specifying precisely the limited extent of police powers of arrest and stop and search, and the boundaries of the necessary minimum of justifiable police coercion. Alongside such changes it will be necessary to introduce new laws on the admissibility of evidence and to assert – what is still formally the case in Scotland – that the judiciary have a key role in controlling police behaviour.

A government which seeks to counter crime must start by guaranteeing the effectiveness of policing, which means asserting the primacy of democracy in the criminal justice system – a democratic magistracy and judiciary as much as a democratic police. But political and legal reform alone will never be sufficient. The internal organization and culture of the police must be radically reworked to give priority to what is presently dismissed as 'minor' and 'trivial'. Specialization and claims to professional expertise and exclusive knowledge must give way to a recognition that crime detection and control require, above all, an ability to communicate, to exchange information and to treat people as equals. Hence the need radically to reorganize the police, to abolish the unnecessary specialist departments and squads, and to give priority to the less glamorous but most urgent taks of routine crime detection and control.

In essence, effective policing necessitates public support, and it is only a police force which positively pursues civil liberties within the context of democratic accountability that will ever gain that confidence. In this context we have examined in detail the problems of police discretion and the politics of policing, and outlined our conception of minimal policing. However, it is important to reiterate that we do not see 'better policing' by itself as the answer to the problem of crime. It is only one part of a series of institutional changes and reforms that are required – in the courts, the prisons and in social work. So saying, it has to be recognized that the police are necessary and that a minimum level of coercion is an inevitable feature of social order. Nonetheless we have not argued for more police – with greater public confidence and greater respect for the public, we could cope with less. We do not want to extend the role of the police, but to restrict it. We are not anti-police, just totally against undemocratic forms of policing.

Law and order cannot be treated as an issue on its own. In the inner cities crime is *the* social problem, second only to unemployment. It is the problem of the poor, the weak and the vulnerable. For them, losing the fight against crime is the worst crime of all.

Bibliography

Alderson, J. 1985: *Law and Disorder*. London: Hamish Hamilton.

Baldwin, R., and Kinsey, R. 1982: *Police Powers and Politics*. London: Quartet Books.

— 1985: Rules, Realism and the Police Act. *Critical Social Policy*, Spring.

Black, D. 1980: *The Manners and Customs of the Police*. New York: Free Press.

Bottomley, K. and Coleman, C. 1981: *Understanding Crime Rates*. Farnborough: Gower.

Bramshill 1982: *Crime Prevention, a Co-ordinated Approach*, proceedings of a seminar on crime prevention. Police Staff College, Bramshill.

Bridges, L. 1982: Keeping the lid on: British urban policy 1976–81. *Race and Class*, vol. 23, no. 2/3.

Buck, M., et al. 1983: *Crime Prevention Diversion: Corporate Action with Juveniles*, proceedings of a conference in Birmingham, December.

Bunyan, T. 1976: *The Political Police in Britain*. London: Quartet Books.

Burrows, J. and Tarling, R. 1982: *Clearing Up Crime*. London: HMSO.

Campbell, D. 1979: Society under surveillance. In P. Hain et al., *Policing the Police*. London: Calder.

Christian, L. 1983: *Policing by Coercion*. London: GLC.

Clarke, R., and Hough, M. 1984: *Crime and Police Effectiveness*. London: Home Office Research Unit.

Clarke, R. 1980: Situational crime prevention: theory and practice. *British Journal of Criminology*, vol. 20, no. 2, pp. 136–47.

Critchley, T. 1978: *A History of the Police in England and Wales*. London: Constable.

Faragher, T. 1985: The police response to violence against women in the home. In J. Pahl (ed.), *Private Violence and Public Policy*. London: Routledge and Kegan Paul.

Gilroy, P., and Sim, J. 1985: Law and order: the state of the left. *Capital and Class*, Summer.

GLC 1983: *Report of the Panel of Inquiry into Racial Harassment.*
— 1984: *Report of the Panel of Inquiry into Vandalism in London.*
— 1985: *Reorganisation of the Metropolitan Police.* GLC Police Committee report.
Hall, R., 1985: *Ask Any Woman: A London Inquiry into Rape and Sexual Assault.* Bristol: Falling Wall Press.
Hanmer, J. and Saunders, S. 1984: *Well Founded Fear: A Community Study of Violence to Women.* London: Hutchinson.
Home Office 1975: Criminal Investigation Project, Home Office Police Research Services (unpublished).
— 1981: *Racial Attacks.*
— 1982: *Criminal Statistics for England and Wales.*
— 1983a: *Crime Reduction*, an interdepartmental group report on crime.
— 1983b: *Draft Circular on Crime Prevention.*
— 1984a: *Criminal Justice: A Working Paper.*
— 1984b: *Neighbourhood Watch, A Note on Implementation.*
Hough, M. 1980: *Uniformed Police Work and Management Technology.* London: Home Office Research Unit.
Hough, M. and Mayhew, P. 1983: *The British Crime Survey.* London: Home Office Research Unit.
— 1985: *Taking Account of Crime: Key Findings from the 1984 British Crime Survey.* London: HMSO
Jones, M. 1980: *Organisational Aspects of Police Behaviour.* Farnborough: Gower.
Kinsey, R. 1984: *The Merseyside Crime Survey*, First report. Merseyside Metropolitan Council
— 1985a: *The Survey of Merseyside Police Officers*, First report. Merseyside Metropolitan Council.
— 1985b: *Crime and Policing on Merseyside*, Final report. Merseyside Metropolitan Council.
Landau, H. 1981: Juveniles and the police. *British Journal of Criminology*, vol. 21, pp. 143–72.
Lea, J. and Young, J. 1984: *What Is To Be Done About Law and Order?* Harmondsworth: Penguin Books.
Mark, R. 1978: *In the Office of Constable.* London: Constable.
Mawby, R. 1979: *Policing The City.* Farnborough: Gower.
McCabe, S. and Sutcliffe, F. 1978: *Defining Crime: A Study of Police Decisions.* Oxford: Blackwell.
McClintock, D. and Avison, N. 1968: *Crime in England and Wales.* London: Heinemann.
McNee, D. 1979: *McNee's Law.* London: Constable.
Morris, P. and Heal, K. 1981: *Crime Control and the Police.* London: Home Office Research Unit.

Newman, K. 1983: *Report of the Commissioner of Police of the Metropolis for the Year 1982*. Cmnd.8928. London: HMSO.

Nicholson, M. 1979: *The Yorkshire Ripper*. London: Allen and Unwin.

Pitts, J. 1979: Changes in the Control of Youthful Disorder in England and Wales (unpublished report).

Pollock, J. 1983: *Reducing Crime in America: The Figgie Report*. New York: Figgie International.

PSI 1983: *Police and People in London:*
  vol. 1. D. Smith: *A Survey of Londoners;*
  vol. 2. S. Small: *A Group of Young Black People;*
  vol. 3. D. Smith: *A Survey of Police Officers;*
  vol. 4. D. Smith and J. Gray: *The Police in Action*. London: The Policy Studies Institute.

Reiner, R. 1978: *The Blue-Coated Worker*. Cambridge University Press.

Ryan, M. and Sim, J. 1984: Decoding Leon Brittan. *The Abolitionist*, no. 16.

Scarman 1981: *The Scarman Report*. Cmnd.8427. London: HMSO.

Skogan, W. 1983: *Communities and Crime*. New York: Wiley.

Sparks et al. 1977: *Surveying Victims*. Chichester: Wiley.

Spencer, S. 1985: The eclipse of the police authority. In B. Fine and R. Millar (eds), *Policing the Miners' Strike*. London: Lawrence and Wishart.

Walker, N. 1971: *Crimes, Courts and Figures*. Harmondsworth: Penguin Books.

Wilson, J. 1968: *Varieties of Police Behavior*. Cambridge, Mass.: Harvard University Press.

Wilson, J and Kelling, G. 1982: Broken Windows. *Atlantic Monthly*, March, pp. 29–38.

Young, J. 1971: The police as amplifiers of deviancy. In S. Cohen (ed.), *Images of Deviance*. Harmondsworth: Penguin Books.

Index